SHINE

and don't give a

SHITE

SHINE

and don't give a

SHITE

Own Your Light, Share Your Divine Soul Gifts
& Live a Magical Life. Without Apology.

Kirsty Caló

Dedication

This book is dedicated to my beautiful daughters Liberty and Georgia (who was still snuggled in my tummy during the final months of writing this book!)

Thank you for choosing me, thank you for loving me and thank you for reminding me just how magical life can be!

My wish is that you will always feel free to be yourself and shine brightly, no matter what.

All my love,

Contents

Contents

Contents

Contents

"Champion the right to be yourself; dare to be different and to set your own pattern, live your own life, and follow your own star."

Wilferd Peterson

Making Your Way Through the Book

You will notice that the book is mainly split into five core parts, with the focal point of each part corresponding to a letter in the word **SHINE**, as follows:

Stop (Part One)

Honour (Part Two)

Illuminate (Part Three)

Nurture (Part Four)

Expand (Part Five)

I decided to lay the book out this way because 1) I was utterly obsessed with acrostic poems as a kid; and 2) to give it a format that is easy to follow (but mostly coz of the acrostic thing.)

You will notice that throughout the book I have included **SHINE A LIGHT** prompts which are opportunities for you to pause and reflect on how what I've been blabbing on about might relate to your own life and journey.

You might wanna have a journal, notepad or something to write notes on so that you can record your reflections or, instead of writing notes, you might choose to adapt the exercises to suit your own preferences.

The most important thing is to actually take the time to pause and reflect on the exercises as they arise. Taking in the information is one thing but actually *doing* the activities will take you to a whole new level.

As you open up to moving past your comfort zone you will connect with yourself deeper than you may have for a long time, if not ever before. This is not only because of the magic that I have personally weaved into each page of this book (wink-wink!) but because you are choosing to take your life to a whole new place of allowing and <u>that</u> is magical.

That being said, if you really don't feel ready to do every single exercise please don't force yourself. The most important thing is that you look after your wellbeing and follow your own intuition. It could be that you are not quite meant to venture into that part yet and you can always re-visit later.

Also, please bear in mind that this book is in no way intended to replace any professional medical advice, diagnosis or treatment. If you have any specific concerns, please seek advice from an appropriate healthcare representative.

This Book is For Us

When I began my spiritual awakening journey, I had no frigging clue what was going on and had no one to really turn to to ask what the frig was going on.

I am writing this book for the me who really needed to be shown the way when I had no clue where I was going. I am also writing this book for you because I want to remind you that it is safe to be a bright light in the world.

It is safe to let go of the things that you cannot control so that you can focus your energy on being so uniquely YOU that you can serve yourself, your family and the world in the way that only YOU can.

You are here to be YOU in all your magnificent glory.

Being YOU (when you are embracing your truth, your gifts, your light and all the magical aspects of your life) will look like more JOY and ABUNDANCE and LOVE and FREEDOM and SUCCESS than you could shake a stick at.

I believe that we are all meant to thrive, to be happy and free.

It's your birthright. It's who you truly are. It's why you are here.

When you cut yourself off from that, you feel the pain of it. The pain that is telling you that you are not being true to yourself.

By reclaiming your light, you are reclaiming Your Divine Essence and the cool consequence of this is that you get to live the most incredibly magical life in the process.

But first, you gotta let go of any notion that you shining and being you is somehow the equivalent of you being a selfish, smug, sparkly arsehole. It really is not.

Shining at your BRIGHTEST most RADIANT capacity depletes no one or nothing. So why on Earth would you ever dim your light?

By being fully you, you get to impact the world in incredible ways that only you can.

So don't allow anyone to shame you for shining and being as radiant as you are. It's ok for you to be as happy and as free and as abundant and as successful as you desire.

We are shifting into a new paradigm and you are being invited to be unapologetically YOU in all your glory because, after all, that's why you came.

Your time is now, and I'm so excited to share in your journey.

All my love,

The Tale of Her Magical Awakening

Once upon a time, a girl who had been (for way too long)
conforming, fitting the mould, following the rules and carrying
the weight of the *should-ers* on her shoulders, decided,
once-and-for-all-and-finally that

enough was enough.

She vowed from that day forward that she would no longer try
to stuff her gorgeous, brilliant light into the dullest,
darkest box. A box that had been splintered by the tiniest of
cracks formed from the shame, sadness, guilt and hurt which
only allowed her to SHINE a sliver at a time.

She vowed to let go of caring about what everyone else thought
or felt about her and instead chose to, from that day forward,
listen to her DIVINE truth.

The seat of her own infinite, inner wisdom, forged over many
lifetimes, yet often neglected by her in her quest to be *everything
to everyone.*

She vowed to give up her need to please others *no matter what.*
A natural tendency that had forced her so far down her list of
priorities that she barely recognised or remembered her own
desires or sense of self.

She vowed to follow the beat of her own heart and love herself,

Unconditionally.

She vowed to stand tall and proud and powerful,

Unapologetically.

She vowed to let her radiance illuminate the world,

Unashamedly.

She would rest in the eternal knowledge that despite the
fiercest of fears and deepest of doubts, she was, in fact, enough.
That she had always been enough, and she would forever be
enough.

And just like that, she boldly, and oh so bravely, stepped right
out into the world again. Into the most beautiful and magical,
rainbow-tinged sunset that she had ever witnessed, and she
lived happily ever after.

The Beginning...

First
Things
First

To No Longer Giving a Shite

Thank you so much for choosing my book. I am so grateful that you are here and I am very excited to share my journey from being a fully-fledged people-pleaser to a pretty much fully recovered ex-sufferer of *giveashiteitis.*

I now spend my days happily shining my light, sharing my soul gifts, living my life, being myself and flipping the (proverbial) bird to anyone who has a problem with it.

By the way, you'd be forgiven for having no prior knowledge of the term *giveashiteitis* because, you'll be shocked to learn, it is a totally made-up word.

Nonetheless, the effects of *giveashiteitis* are devastating. It is the number one basher of **dreams**, killer of **magic** and dimmer of **light**.

I realised that I had been suffering from this common (but often untreated) ailment for most of my life, and the older I got the more aware of it I became. It caused me to hide and shrink and deny who I was, and it was the reason I resisted fully shining my light.

It was only through a truly awakening conversation with my dear friend, Maria, back in October 2017, that I realised just how much my attachment to people-pleasing was stifling me.

I was so frustrated to, at 38 years old, still be living my life according to what I felt I *should* be doing rather than just following my heart and sharing more of myself with the world.

As we were wrapped in a back and forth conversation I, in frustration and with an utter sense of *enough is a friggin' nuff*, blurted something out along the lines of:

I wish I could just shine and not give a shite!

As I said these words out loud to Maria, the impact of them hit me like the pain of a bare foot stood on a pile of Lego bricks.

I realised that I had wasted *so much* precious time and energy trying to be accepted and validated by others as if their opinions of me not only mattered more than mine, but also determined the extent to which I was worthy.

I was ready to let go of all of that noise. I was well and truly ready to stop giving a shite.

But I knew that if I *really* wanted to pursue my dream of living a life true to myself, I would first have to deal with the persistent pain-in-the-backside thought that was actually causing me to hold myself back.

It is, in fact, a very common thought that so many of us walk around with each and every day, totally unaware of how its sneaky presence is, in fact, sabotaging the heck out of our lives.

I've heard these words muttered under the breath of someone who even remotely thinks about tip-toeing out of their comfort zone. It's *this* thought:

What will they think of me?

This thought (or variations of it) had for so long piped up just at those crucial moments in my life when I was on the brink of stepping out and doing something rather marvellous and courageous.

Sometimes the *they* was specific to a particular person or group. Other times it was just a generic *they* (as in the whole world).

You'd be mistaken if you're thinking that I was, in fact, some egotistical, self-obsessed maniac because, in reality, this thought had little to do with me being adored or put on some kind of pedestal and much more to do with this need to simply *belong*.

I also had this feeling that the more I lived my life, floating around doing my own thing, the more it irritated some people. As if they were always thinking: *why can't you just be normal?*

I was caught between the rock and the hard place of wanting to fit in and wanting to just be freely me. Of wanting to be accepted but feeling that I would have to dim and hide my light and my true self in order to be.

I had a deep, and I mean *deeeeep,* belief that told me if I allowed myself to fulfill all of my heart's desires and live the most magical life, some people would hate me for it. That they would feel pissed off and that I would be the one *responsible* for making them feel bad.

I'd seen it happen before. I'd been around people who had scoffed and rolled their eyes and outwardly expressed their own envy when someone they perceived as being more beautiful or happier or more successful or wealthier crossed their path.

I had seen other women grouping together to whisper and talk crap about another woman who dared to shine brighter than them. As if that person who they deemed as being *too much* served as a painful reminder of how they had allowed themselves to shrink and hide their own brilliance.

So the people-pleaser in me, and the me that so desperately wanted to be accepted and belong, would rather that others feel happy and feel good, even if it was at the expense of my own sense of freedom. I would dim simply to not be rejected, and it felt like a worthy price to pay. Until it wasn't.

Seriously, how messed up is that? Why would my happiness be less important than anybody else's anyway? Why would I choose to be around those who mocked or ridiculed or shamed me in the first place?

As I got older, the thought was less dominant in my day to day life and often times I could shake it off. I could actually be defiant in my right to be who I was and literally not worry if it triggered or upset anyone because, why the hell should it?

But it was when I knew I would have to be bolder and more unapologetically me that the *what will they think?* thought became particularly rambunctious.

Just as I was about to put myself out there and do something super courageous, that sneaky little thought would saunter over all cool and collected and piss all over my self-confidence parade, whilst leaving me mad at *myself* for not packing my piss-proof umbrella.

It would have me doubting myself and my plans at every chance it could.

But something *was* shifting because I had found a way to keep moving forward regardless. To keep challenging myself irrespective of how scared I felt.

I had already established my own business helping people get clear on what they wanted from life and how to achieve it. I had already created and hosted a number of my own workshops and online courses as well as selling spaces on my group and one-to-one programmes.

I was fortunate to have built a growing audience of amazing people all over the world, who shared my videos and messages with enthusiasm, and I began to see that I had a real gift with helping others create happier lives.

But I began to realise that, although my work had been impactful, it had reached a plateau. I no longer felt inspired to just share the basics of what I knew. There was way more I had learned and I knew it was part of my mission to share it with others. Even if I knew it was waaaaaay out there.

Along my own spiritual journey, I learned that when we connect to our own inner light (which looks basically like being 100000% you and doing stuff that brings out your true self) we tap into a flow of energy that allows us to **co-create** our reality.

When we are fully aligned with our light and who we truly are the most magical experiences and blessings flow to us, abundantly and with a sense of ease. When we are fully connected to our light, we are, in fact, connected to our deepest essence, our soul, our spirit.

I refer to this aspect of each of us as **Your Infinite Self** or **Your Divine Essence** and it is the part of you that is just that...both Infinite and Divine (Infinite meaning: *eternal* and Divine meaning: *of God*).

You are a spark of that Divinity and you are created from and always connected to The Universal Flow.

To me, The Universal Flow (which is The Universe, God, Source) is the never-ending stream of loving, creative, life-force energy that is responsible for both regulating the tides of the ocean and regulating your breathing when you sleep oh-so-soundly in your bed.

It's the energy that flows through me as I connect intuitively with those who choose to work with me and about whom I am able to pick up incredible insights. When things I couldn't possibly have known about them just come to me *like magic*.

Shine And Don't Give A Shite

It's the energy that wells up inside me (as a mixture of love and pride) when I see my daughter playing or being lost in the moment, picking daisies and chasing butterflies and reminding me that I too can enter that same magical flow at any time.

It's that energy that was calling me to be more *me,* and when I did, it would flood my life with abundant blessings and magical happenings.

And, as weird as this sounds, it was that energy that freaked me waaaaaay out.

I really couldn't explain it at the time, but I had this resistance to allowing myself to be connected to the energy constantly.

When I thought about this deep, infinite energy, which I knew was responsible for these seemingly new-found spiritual gifts that I had access to, it felt too much.

I was aware that there was something so big and expansive and unknown in it. It felt like an overwhelming sense of awe and wonderment. A bit like the feeling I get when I step into a high-vaulted, echo-y cathedral or other place of worship, or look out at a massive expanse of land, taking in the epic-ness of it all.

So I shrank away from the energy, and in doing so, shrank away from myself, and in doing so, suppressed a lot of my own energy and my zest for life.

Deep down, though, it was as if this feeling of *too-much-ness* that I felt when I tapped into The Universal Flow, was actually to do with how I felt about myself.

I know that when I am fully connected to this incredible energy I feel like there's nothing that I cannot do. When I am aligned to that energy my life becomes a series of unexplainable magical moments after another.

I feel braver and stronger and more confident. I regain my power and, essentially, I stop giving a shite about trying to please others by staying small and sweet and agreeable. I allow myself to be fully me in all of my glory and what I create from that space just seems to flow through me with ease.

And that's why I was afraid of fully embodying the energy. It felt too much for the part of me that believed that life has to have comfort zones never to be crossed.

And most of all, I was scared about what I would become if I allowed that energy to flow through me all the time.

Who would I be if I wasn't Kirsty, the people-pleaser with zero boundaries who just lives her life according to what she feels she should do? To quote my mum, Mary:

What the frig??

Was I *seriously* going to spend my life bowing to this ridiculous notion that I had to hold myself back in order to please others?

One day I realised that all of the fears were not only holding me back from sharing my unique blend of magic with the world (something we all possess), they were actually holding me back from being freely me.

Shine And Don't Give A Shite

I decided right there and then, and once and for all, that it really was time to stop giving so much attention and energy to things that I just could not control and instead get the frig on with embracing my inner light and living my most magical life, regardless of what others would think.

So I set out to write this book, but time and time again I came up against the same inner resistance.

I was intent on writing a book all about overcoming *giveashiteitis* while still totally suffering from it myself.

The irony of wishing to write a book about not giving a shite about what others think *whilst* 100000% worrying about what others would think was not lost on me!

But the opportunity to finally get the heck over my crap wasn't lost on me either. I knew that this book was going to be the healer for me before it could even remotely help anyone else.

I knew that actually sharing my honest truth in indelible, permanent, forever in print, black and white was EXACTLY what I needed to do.

I knew that this book would be a catalyst in helping me overcome my tendency to give a shite about things that are, quite frankly, a waste of my mother-loving time, energy and attention. Once and for all.

Because enough was enough. It was time to walk my talk.

So here I am, sharing my most honest truths in the form of this book. Walking my talk.

This book is based on my personal lived experience and my experience of working with people from all over the world who have also suffered from *giveashiteitis*. This book will support you in owning your light and shining beautifully, boldly and brightly. This book will guide you in creating a clear vision of what your magical life will look like, and it will help you in allowing it to unfold.

But this book will not tell you anything that you don't already know on a deep soul level. This book really serves as a reminder of a truth that you have sensed all you your life, but perhaps have never understood consciously.

The truth that you were born to be truly you and thrive in magical ways. The truth that you were born to LIGHT UP the world with the Divine Soul Gifts you were born with.

Through your art.

Through your music.

Through your words.

Through your healing.

Through your intuition.

Through your teaching.

Through your wisdom.

Through your love.

Through your light.

And trust me when I say that life will keep calling you to rise up and share your true self with the world because no amount of resistance will hold you away from being who you really ARE...

So, it's time to LET GO of the stories that say you *can't* or *shouldn't* or *mustn't* be as bold as you really are and show us your **true colours.**

Because, if you wish to be fully you (which will look like completely owning your light, sharing your gifts and living an awesomely magical life in the process) you have to heal any *giveashiteitis* you may be currently suffering from, and that can only be done once you decide...

to let go of worrying about what everyone else thinks of you.

Let me say that again for those at the back.

If you really wanna live a life that is 100000000% true to you, you have to stop giving a shite about what others think of you.

There really is no other way.

Because, let's be honest, trying to live freely whilst worrying incessantly about what every human in the entire history of the planet has to say about it, do not a good mix make. It was only when I completely *got* this (like a long-overdue cosmic smack upside the head) did my life really start to take magical turn upon magical twist.

I began to thrive in all ways.

My health started to improve. I felt generally better than I had ever felt in my life. I felt more connected to myself and had more clarity than ever about my purpose.

I became a more present and playful mum to my lovely daughter, Liberty. I started to lose physical, emotional and metaphorical weight that I had been holding on to for years.

I stopped doing things out of obligation or people-pleasing. I stopped shrinking my success and instead celebrated myself more confidently and without apology.

I allowed myself to invest in things that supported my wellbeing such as good food, Pilates and yoga classes, massages, healing sessions, fun trips away, retreats, meditation classes and other things that nourished my mind, body and soul.

I allowed myself to **be** the magnetic manifestor that I knew I truly was and incredible things started lining up seemingly *out of the blue* because I was no longer doubting my worthiness to receive.

I fully embraced a feeling of ease and flow that I had been resisting forever, and in doing so, gave up my attachment to struggle. I let go of anything that was holding me back from being truly me. I created a shed load of new personal boundaries and started saying NOOOOOOOO! I also made a commitment to pursue things that used to terrify the living daylights out of me (such as writing the book you're reading right now!)

Shine And Don't Give A Shite

I began to share my message with more confidence and less fear of judgement. I began the process of relearning to trust myself and follow my intuition, rather than being negatively influenced by anything outside of myself.

Above all else, I consciously decided to just embrace all parts of me. I allowed myself to actually **live**, and I finally stopped fretting about what anyone had to say about it (well, for the most part anyway!).

I share all of this because I want to make it clear that I didn't *make* all of this stuff happen. It was the natural effect of doing the **inner work** that I will share with you in this book.

Through doing that work you will begin to uncover any funky beliefs that may be making it difficult for you to fully shine and embrace your inner magic. It will help you identify what you really desire for your life as well as help you to see what is currently holding you back from allowing it in. All the doubt and fear and limiting beliefs that have, up until now, made you believe you are less than you are.

It's time to let go of all of that and this book will show you how. I will remind you just how truly remarkable you really are so that you can begin to live a magical life that totally lights you (and the world) up.

But know this: **wherever you are in your life at this precise moment is perfect for you right now.** Trust your journey, trust the process and above ALL else:

trust yourself.

So, if you have spent way too much of your life worrying about what others think, to the point of hiding and shrinking yourself, your gifts and your light...

this book is for you.

If you have felt afraid to share the success in your life because you feel that it will make others reject you...

this book is for you.

If you know that you have MAGIC within you that you are keeping contained because you don't want to be *too much*...

this book is for you.

I've written it to help you realise that you no longer need to dim any aspect of you, and to remind you that it is safe to embrace all parts of yourself, without apology. And to help you understand that you being fully you will not only impact *your* life in magical ways, but it will also have a massively positive effect on the lives of those around you -- and the world!

But as much as I can share my experience and wisdom, it's up to you to make the commitment to yourself to use this book as a catalyst to transform your life, if that's what you want.

Because, let's be honest. When was the last time that you read a book like this and then promptly doubted whether what was being shared could really work for **you**?

Well, if you are anything like me, you are an eternal seeker of little nuggets of wisdom and you are constantly seeking the answer to a question that, although you can't fully articulate it, goes something like: *What is the one thing I need to know, the secret sauce, the undiscovered answer that will finally, finally, FINALLY help me to get the heck over my stuckness?*

And so you search and search and search and search, and you devour all the tips you can from every nook and cranny but still, you feel unsatisfied. Why?

Because you are not fully listening to yourself.

I know, I know; that's not always easy but it will get easier and easier the more you explore the aspects of yourself that you have hidden away for so long.

I'll be honest, sometimes the work can sting like hell. It can be painful to really look at all the ways you may have been giving your power away or not honouring yourself. But I encourage you to make a promise that you will be as kind and compassionate with yourself as you can possibly be.

Over time you will find the layers of limiting beliefs, doubts and fears will just start to release and peel away, just like the papery layers of an onion, and as with any onion peeling, it really is normal to expect to shed a few tears along the way.

Shine And Don't Give A Shite

My Divine Wake-Up Call

It was a wintery-cold Sunday evening back in October 2013 and I was lying alone in my bed, fully believing that I was dying. I had no idea what was actually happening to me but I was unable to move any part of my body.

I had come over a bit strange earlier that evening so I told my husband, Enrico, that I was gonna get an early night and snooze away what I assumed was just a case of massive sleep deprivation.

It made sense to be that. After all, Libby was just 16 months old at the time and sleeping through the night was a rarity for her or us. I'd also had an exceptionally full-on week work wise.

As I lay there, beyond exhausted but unable to nod off, I realised that there was way more going on than just needing a good night's kip.

Unable to breathe, I felt my body start to become very still and then, as surreal as it sounds, I heard a faint whisper inside that told me to *just surrender...*

So I did. I had no choice. (By the way, it wasn't an *actual* whisper coz that sounds creepy as all hell. It was more of a deep inner knowing that was gently reassuring me that everything was, despite appearances, going to be ok.)

And even though my human brain was wondering what the actual frig *was* going on, that deeper more connected whispering part of me actually *did* know what the frig was going on.

It literally felt like I was having some kind of out-of-body experience and it was like nothing I'd felt before. I still couldn't move or speak or call out, but I felt oddly calm.

After what felt like an eternity spent wondering whether I was just about to take my last breath, I realised what was happening. I was being forced to STOP. Literally.

Some may have called what was happening in that moment a Divine *Intervention*. To me, it felt like a Divine *Wake-Up Call*. An incessant alarm that had been ringing in my ears for years and years, but one that I could no longer ignore.

I had, after all, been ignoring it for way too long.

I had been pushing and going until I could go no more.

I was being forced to stop before I literally burnt out. For good.

I know, I sound (as Enrico would say) like a *drama queen*, but the years that have followed since that night have taught me that episodes like this *are* pretty dramatic and they *are* a pretty big deal.

Shine And Don't Give A Shite

When we don't allow ourselves to follow the call of our soul, this kind of thing happens.

When we stay in relationships or habits that are slowly destroying us, this kind of thing happens.

When we are ignoring the signs time and time again (and I'm not just talking about the 11:11 sort that I see ALL the time), this kind of thing will happen.

When we stay in a place of resisting the epic flow of life, this kind of thing happens. And believe me, it is painful.

This incident, I knew, was attributed to the fact that I was overworking myself and I was ignoring my inner knowing that was telling me to slow down and re-evaluate my commitments. But instead of listening I powered on through, working, working, working.

I was out gigging as a professional singer until the early hours most Friday and Saturday nights.

I was running back-to-back vocal coaching sessions on weekday evenings and weekends.

I was also working my day job as a part-time primary school teacher and, in between, being a busy mum to my Libby.

I was juggling, and I was dropping the juggles (or whatever the hell they're called) all over the place.

Time was stretched and so was I. There was no time to create. No time to rest. No time to breathe.

I was heading for Burnout Central at high speed and The Universe had to serve me a wake-up call I **could not** ignore.

It was time to start paying attention and it was time to slow the train before it derailed.

In the days, weeks, months and years that followed, my life shifted dramatically.

I melted like the cackling, green, wicked witch from *The Wizard of Oz* does when Dorothy chucks that bucket of water over her. Many, many tears were shed as many, many feelings were brought to the surface.

It felt as though a tempestuous, emotional whirlwind was raging within me.

I became aware of a deep core belief inside that was telling me **I WAS NOT GOOD ENOUGH** and it was this belief that was keeping me from fully listening to my own inner guidance and following my heart.

I didn't realise it at the time, but the night in question would set into motion the incredible spiritual awakening that led me to writing this book.

I was finally able to see who I truly was under all of the limited beliefs, fears and doubts I had carried around for so long, and I discovered tools that helped me to release what had been holding me back all that time.

It was time to allow my light to fully shine instead of shrinking under the illusion that I was not good enough.

Shine And Don't Give A Shite

I was guided to books, courses, healings and teachings that changed my life (most of which are referenced in the back of this book).

I began to see that I was totally worthy of living a life that lit me up, instead of playing small.

I learned the simple principles of the Law of Attraction and eventually began to manifest my desires into my reality by tapping into the infinite powers that be.

I started to share what I had learned with the world through my online platform, *The Happy Hummingbird*, and had such encouraging feedback from people all over the world who told me how my message was helping them.

I had definitely discovered something magical and I devoured anything I could learn on topics of manifestation, soul healing, meta-physics and the nature of The Universe.

But with this new-found thirst for spiritual knowledge came a growing sense of dissatisfaction. Yes, it was pretty cool to be able to manifest parking spaces, incredible trips abroad, creative ideas that would eventually make me money, a home and so much more but I had this knowing that there was waaaay more to unearth, and I had just skimmed the metaphorical tip of a very big iceberg!

As with my previous experience with this new-found energy, it was overwhelming to me and I would only allow myself to explore it to a small degree.

I was not consistently allowing myself to thrive.

I would have days and weeks of amazing things lining up for me but would counter the *good* that was flowing to me by sabotaging the crap out of it, just as I had always done.

Late nights (and I'm talking, like 3:00 a.m. bedtimes every night -- not pretty when you've got a baby) became my poison of choice.

I also resisted sleep because I knew that if I was dog-tired during the day, my energy could only go towards doing the stuff that I *had* to do to keep my life at a mediocre level and so that there would be no energy left for the expansion my soul was craving.

And because, deep down, there was a part of me that was just not comfortable with living such a happy, free and lit-up life whilst so many others were suffering, struggling, striving and just surviving in the world.

I mean, who was I to live so abundantly, so freely, so happily, so selfishly?

I was plagued by feelings of guilt that I had found the *cheat's way* to happiness and success. I had essentially learned the principles of the Law of Attraction and how to harness it to my advantage. And it was incredible!

Sooooo many amazing things would line up for me just because I'd think about what I desired, line my energy up with it and allow myself to receive it. Literally.

But it was like I hadn't really earned it if I didn't give my blood, sweat and tears to it.

Shine And Don't Give A Shite

I became profoundly aware of deep programming that existed within me (picked up from this lifetime and many, many before) that basically said: *Life has to be a struggle; it has to be hard.*

I also knew that this was just not true. Or, at least, it didn't *have* to be true. Life is not supposed to be a struggle. Of course there are challenges, but I realised that we have a greater power within us that allows us to overcome those challenges.

I knew that life *could* be easier. I had experienced it on so many occasions when I allowed myself to surrender to The Universal Flow.

Others would notice how things just seemed to be working out for me and it was no longer something I could put down to pure coincidence.

It was because, when those things had occurred, I had been connected to My Divine Essence. I had consciously and purposefully co-created the experiences.

But again, it was *too easy.*

I felt uncomfortable with the notion that others around me were working hard to make ends meet while things just seemed to fall into my lap.

I know I must sound like a total plonker. *I mean, who actually does that?*

The fact that I was so determined to sabotage my happiness time and time again was proof that, deep down, I didn't believe it was fair for me to thrive and to have it easy.

So, I would allow myself morsels of goodness, but shut it off before it gathered too much momentum.

Money would come in and then it would be gone. I would feel great in my body and full of vitality but then I'd eat or drink something and I would feel like crap again.

I would feel really amazing about myself and my path, and then I would sit and dwell on all the things that made me a total loser, or why I didn't deserve true happiness or success.

All of this was in a bid to keep me small. To not be that person who everyone hates because they had figured out this secret to *having it all*.

I feared what would happen if I let myself just thrive without breaking the flow of receiving, and moving from one extreme to next was wearing me down.

Inside, I was more anxious than ever.

I had the tools and the knowledge that I needed to fully step into my calling, but I still felt just as stuck as I had been before I received My Divine Wake-Up Call.

It felt horrible. I knew I was more than capable enough to make the changes that I so desired in my life but I also felt as though I was stuck in a permanent straight jacket stitched together by my irrational sense of guilt.

I felt like a fraud. I mean, this was the basis of what I taught, but I was not able to live it.

It felt like I just couldn't allow myself to.

Shine And Don't Give A Shite

I was so overwhelmed by these feelings of intense fear, so wrapped up in these deep, heavy emotions, and it felt like they would never leave.

I started to get that sinking feeling that I would never accomplish any of my hopes and dreams, and that I would push myself into an early grave with the heaviness in my heart and what I was doing to my health in a desperate attempt to avoid myself.

There was a constant battle raging within me.

On one hand I knew that we all have a right to thrive and to live joyous, abundant lives.

But the fearful part of me that was just intent on surviving, that believed life *had* to be stressful would rage back, each time more pissed off at me for daring to believe anything more was available to me.

If you are familiar with the legendary story of *The Two Wolves,* my inner battle will ring true to you.

If you're not, let me share it with you…

Shine And Don't Give A Shite

The Two Wolves

An old Cherokee chief was teaching his grandson about life...

"A fight is going on inside me," he said to the boy.

"It is a terrible fight and it is between two wolves. One is evil. He is anger, envy, sorrow, regret, greed, arrogance, self-pity, guilt, resentment, inferiority, lies, false pride, superiority, self-doubt and ego.

The other is good. He is joy, peace, love, hope, serenity, humility, kindness, benevolence, empathy, generosity, truth, compassion and faith.

This same fight is going on inside you and inside every other person, too."

The grandson thought about it for a minute and then asked his grandfather,

"Which wolf will win?"

The old chief simply replied,

"The one you feed."

I really love this powerful message but I believe that the evil wolf and the good wolf represent something deeper within us. I believe that the battle within us is quite simply between a wolf that *loves* and a wolf that *fears,* and without sounding too cheesy, our life's assignment is to feed the love as much as we can.

Feeding love into your life will look like falling in love with your life, with your deepest desires, with your gifts, with yourself and with your light, and allowing yourself to experience more love in all ways instead of sabotaging yourself.

And...although this may sound like the biggest contradiction ever, it's also time to love your fears, to acknowledge them and to honour that you are feeling how you feel without justification or apology. You can do this without feeding them with more fear but instead by feeding them with LOVE rather than rejecting them or trying to suppress them. *That* is how you begin to transform your life; as I learned for myself.

Our anger, jealousy, sadness, grief and shame are all valid emotions, and the answer, for me, was in actually allowing all of my emotions to be present. To see them, witness them and understand what they were trying to teach me.

When you hold onto emotions rather than expressing them, they begin to control your life. Emotions are meant to flow and they can only do that when you engage with them in a healthy and balanced way. As soon as you try to control or suppress how you feel, you create a resistance to the flow and that resistance controls *you*. I mean, imagine trying to only hold onto positive feelings and doing whatever you could to avoid any negative emotions.

Shine And Don't Give A Shite

It would be so distressing to your wellbeing and it would be contradictory because your motivation for trying to stay positive would be rooted in fear.

Not only that, but how boring would life become?

We are here for all of the emotions, not just the *high vibe* ones.

That's not to say that we can't aim to mainly do things and be around people who make us feel happy and peaceful and joyful. When we allow ourselves to experience more of the vibration of love, our lives become magical beyond measure, but only when doing so is not as an attempt to avoid how we truly feel.

True transformation can only occur when we embrace the contrasting nature of light and darkness. The Yin *and* the Yang.

The key is to acknowledge and accept that, within you, and all of us, there is a wolf that will always feel fear and will always experience emotions that we may have learned are bad or wrong to feel. And, when you realise there are no bad or wrong emotions, you learn to express all emotions in a way that allows you to be free and liberated, not stuck.

By no longer dwelling in the energy of my fears and, instead, acknowledging them and allowing them to move through me, I stopped feeding with more fear and so they were no longer a reason for me to stay small and shrink and hide my true self.

I stopped pushing and I put all my attention and energy into feeling as good in mind, body and soul that I possibly could by releasing anything I had been holding onto.

I surrendered.

I let go of old stories and conditioning and fears and doubts and beliefs that had for so long blocked me from fully tapping into My Divine Essence.

Along the way I could feel the ways I was still trying to resist (cue ridiculously late nights, once again) but I kept moving forward regardless.

I started meditating and journaling every single day. I started connecting with nature, walking, eating well and sleeping (hurrah!), and taking care of my body.

Although, that's not to say that I was able to put myself into some unburstable bubble of happiness and positivity!

I've been met by fear at literally every moment of this awesome journey but the unavoidable truth is this: as long as I am human, there will always be a certain amount of feeding the fearful wolf with more fear that *will* happen.

It's inevitable that if you chose a path of owning your light and living a magical life you will rub up against fear, resentment, self-doubt and a whole host of emotions that so much of the time we try to cram down and avoid.

The sooner you accept that, the smoother your journey will be.

Once I accepted that, I found the sweet spot of balance and I began to release the heavy chains that had been holding me down for so long.

I let go, and in the quiet peacefulness that I had created within myself, I heard the whispers that had guided me all those years before. The day I thought I was dying but later realised I'd actually been reawakening.

It's time to own your light, Kirsty, the whispers told me (again, these really were <u>not</u> creepy whispers).

I listened, and that day I embarked upon a journey of allowing myself to be unapologetically me and live the most lit-up, magical life possible because I understood it was my Divine right to do so. Just as it is yours.

It is my pleasure to share with you all that I have learned along my path in the hope that it will encourage you as you embark on your own journey of coming home to yourself, of owning your light, sharing your soul gifts and living the life you are here to live.

So, are you ready to take your power back?

Are you ready to get really honest about all the ways you've been giving your power away by dimming your light and resisting the magic that wants to flow through you?

...and the ways you have been a passive bystander in your life and allowed yourself to believe you were powerless?

...and how, somewhere along the line, you picked up the belief that it was not safe to be you in all your glory?

Well that's awesome, because this book is *Your* Divine Wake-Up Call...

Part One

Stop

Stop Believing That You Are Powerless

…because you are waaaaaay more powerful than you realise.

We all are.

I believe that when we know that we have access to this deeper power within us, (despite anything that may have already happened or may even be currently happening to us) life gets beyond magical. Not in a rainbows-fairies-butterflies-unicorns kind of way, (although, you know I'm here for *all* of that) but in a way where you discover a hidden depth to yourself that has always been there and you now know how to access.

If you know that you are not living a life that is aligned with your truth, you will probably find that you have been giving your power away.

It usually happens in small, subtle ways. Such as talking badly about yourself or sabotaging your health and success or allowing those around you to diminish your dreams and desires. When you focus on *anything* that someone else thinks, to the degree that it stops you from being who you are, you give your power away.

I can't be me because my family will think I'm too much... (YOU'VE HANDED ALL YOUR POWER OVER TO WHAT YOUR FAMILY THINKS).

I can't share my gifts because society doesn't accept them as normal... (YOU'VE HANDED ALL YOUR POWER OVER TO WHAT SOCIETY DEEMS NORMAL).

I can't live my truth because _____ *will be offended...* (YOU'VE HANDED ALL YOUR POWER OVER TO WHAT _____ CONSIDERS OFFENSIVE).

When you think like this, it reflects a core belief that you have to submit your freedom to everything and anything outside of you, which is a lie.

Of course, this doesn't mean that we should all become set on becoming as power-hungry as we can, abusing and undermining everyone to our own agendas.

That is about control, manipulation, ego and FEAR.

Owning your true power means reconnecting with Your Divine Essence, which is only ever an expression and an extension of LOVE. However, as so many of us have been taught that power is bad and something to be avoided at all costs, we tend to reject our own innate power and therefore our ability to co-create magic and miracles in the process.

There may have also been times in your life when you have felt totally and genuinely dis-empowered.

This can be due to things happening outside of our control or when things happen to us that we feel we are powerless to stop.

As you move through your healing journey, you may find yourself remembering such occurrences in your life and it might suddenly become clear why you have been feeling so powerless for so long.

All I can say is really, really honour that part of your journey and know that it is safe to feel and heal those wounds because healing really is the most vital component to allowing yourself to feel powerful once more.

I can totally understand why, if you have felt disempowered, it can feel easier to give your power away rather than owning it, because owning it fully means taking responsibility for **everything** that comes with it.

It means standing up for what you believe in and speaking your absolute truth.

It means owning all of your gifts and your abilities without apologising for them.

It means following Your Unique Calling and being who you are here to be in the world.

It means loving yourself so fully that others have no choice but to honour you and your boundaries.

It means no longer dimming your light to fit in.

It means remembering that you are an extension of The Infinite and Divine Flow that creates galaxies, stars and magic.

When I re-awoke to My Divine Essence and allowed myself to believe in what was possible for me, I began to feel this shift occurring on such a huge level, and the part of me that had always been so willing to give my power away was overtaken by the part of me that knew I had the right to own every aspect of myself.

I had the power to influence my life in such incredible ways, if only I would stop pretending to be so small and insignificant. I could no longer deny that I was the only one responsible for my life and it was time to take full ownership of that fact instead of giving my power away by believing I had to.

Believe me when I say that, once you see this for yourself, you will already be halfway there. The other half of the journey is choosing to (as much as possible) listen only to the voices, beliefs, people and stories that **support** you.

You will realise that if you believe you are powerless, you will feel powerless and you will remain so. You will also realise that when you allow yourself to be who your truly are and share what you are here to share, you will automatically tune into your powerfulness and *that's* when everything changes.

In order to actually SHINE and not give a SHITE, it is going to take for you to reclaim Your Divine Essence and to feel absolutely amazing about stepping into your greatness, sharing your gifts, shining your light and living the most uplifted and magical life. No matter what anyone else thinks about that.

Because you are a Spark of the Divine!

You are not here by accident.

You have not been put on this incredible planet merely to eke out your days doing things that you hate and spending time with people who do not support who you truly are.

You did not come to play small and shrink, and give all your power away to your perceived limitations.

DEEP DOWN, YOU KNOW THIS.

It's gonna take for you to fully reclaim and OWN the part of yourself that is strong and **powerful** and courageous more than the part of yourself that believes it is not enough or that it is weak or **powerless**.

It's safe for you to be the most amazing, magnificent, magical, expansive, joyful, liberated you that you can possibly be.

It's safe for you to let go of anything or anyone that would rather see you staying in a place of powerlessness or is threatened by you evolving beyond *their* perceived limitations.

It's safe to believe that more is meant for you, and it's safe to live a life that uplifts you and the planet.

It's safe to reclaim your power. Every damn drop of it.

SHINE A LIGHT

How have you been giving your power away?

"You've always had the power, my dear. You just had to learn it for yourself."

Glinda, The Good Witch

(The Wizard of Oz)

Shine And Don't Give A Shite

Stop Putting Yourself Last

…because you are just as important as everyone else.

If, like me, you have been suffering from *giveashiteitis* (or it's more common name: people-pleasing-syndrome) for most of your life, you will find that you have long since been ignoring your own needs and desires.

Often this happens because we are so busy trying to put others first that we just forget that we are important, too.

Sometimes this will look like not taking care of your wellbeing. Maybe you run yourself into the ground rushing from here to there and back again so that you can help others out, all the while stressing yourself out to the max.

You don't like to say no so *of course* you agree to accommodating everyone else's needs so that you don't come across as an unhelpful git.

That's not to say that helping others is wrong, but if you find that you have over-committed yourself, your time and your energy, you will slowly but surely burn yourself full out.

As weird as this sounds, people-pleasers can often times find themselves waiting for something like that to happen so that they finally have a reason to **say no**. So that the saying no was done *for* them.

Now, I know that might sound really ridiculous, but to someone who spent a huge proportion of her life believing that the needs of others were more important than her own, I can verify that when you have a deep belief that the needs of others are more important than your own, saying *no* is a huge challenge.

It can also have very little to do with being pressured by others. Of course, there are some people who absolutely manipulate the good hearts of those willing to bend over backwards to help them, but mostly I have found that the people-pleaser just wants to be so accepted and loved that they will seek out ways in which they can help, whatever the cost and almost always to their own detriment.

Here's the thing. If you really want to be totally true to you, you have to stop putting your needs last and (GASP!!) put your needs first!! I know that is horrifying.

Your instant thought may be: *Well, that's all well and good, Kirsty, but what happens to my kids, my partner, my job, my home, my family, my friends, my pets, my neighbour, my neighbour's cousins and my milkman if I put myself first?*

To which I would answer: *They will be just fine.* In fact, I will go as far to say that you taking care of yourself first will have the most positive impact on those around you.

My daughter, Libby, absolutely benefits more from me looking after myself rather than being so busy and run down and overcommitted that I can hardly be present with her. That was by far the biggest lesson that My Divine Wake-Up Call taught me—that frazzled, frantic, burned-out mummy is not the lasting memory I wanted Libby to have from her childhood.

Unfortunately, it took for me to almost push myself into an early grave by trying to keep all the plates above my head spinning, before I learned that it was no way to live.

It was only when I started to put my needs **first** that every area of my life changed for the better. It improved even more when I no longer felt guilty about doing so. I mean, why should I feel guilty for taking care of myself?

And you know what? I am done with the perpetuated bullshit that says putting yourself first is selfish and greedy and wrong.

Nothing could be further from the truth and the sooner you realise this, the better your life will become in all areas. Over time you will no longer see your value as being based on how accommodating and available and attentive you can be for every single person you know.

And when that happens you will be able to fully see yourself as someone truly worthy because you and your needs really do matter.

SHINE A LIGHT

Where in your life are you putting the needs of others first at the absolute expense of yourself?

Stop Seeking External Validation

…because only you possess the answers you seek.

Have you ever considered doing something bold, courageous or seemingly against the grain, but stop yourself in your tracks when you consider what others would think about you if you actually did it? All of a sudden that feeling of enthusiasm and passion gets drowned out by doubt and a firm sense of resistance. It is that resistance that stops so many of us from actually going after our dreams and daring to follow the path that we are being called towards.

Needing others to approve of you before you do the things that you know would light you up and make your heart sing is the biggest trap ever, because, it's only what you think and feel about yourself that will ever give you that sense of validation that you seek. Yet, somewhere along the way, we pick up a belief that it's only ever external validation that matters and, before long, we stop trusting our own guidance system.

It's why we allow others to talk us out of following our own intuition, believing instead that their opinions and beliefs are more valid and reliable than our own.

Shine And Don't Give A Shite

And, it's the biggest cause of *giveashiteitis* in people-pleasers all over the world.

Side note: I do think some things do warrant a wee bit of friendly intervention. Like the time you insisted on having your holiday romance's name tattooed up your wedding ring finger, while enjoying a very drunken last night in Corfu.

Yes, that's definitely one for the: *What on earth are you thinking?* category, and any friend who talks you out of that is a keeper.

However, when you seek validation from others about things that you already know are right for you, it invalidates how you truly feel about pursuing those things that make you feel alive and creative and free.

Those things that you know are your calling, your path, your destiny, your truth.

It's those awe-inspiring, heart-skip-a-beat-inducing things that make you remember WHO you are and WHY you are here.

It's those things that connect you back to Your Divine Essence.

Maybe it's writing that book you've been planning for years. Or quitting your job you hate and deciding to start a business doing what you love. Or selling your house and deciding to go on a one-year adventure around the globe. Or anything that feels like a massive leap out of your comfort zone.

So, full of excitement, you share your vision with someone you feel will be equally as excited for you, but instead they try to tell you all the reasons why you should in fact *not* do what you desire and why you'd be foolish to even think about doing such a thing.

And because you have this majorly irritating and deeply intrinsic impulse to take their opinion (hell, *anyone's* opinion) over your own, you start to think; *maybe they're right.* And back down poop mountain your plans slide.

If you find yourself constantly looking to others for guidance (even when there is a pulsating, eager and resonant YES coming from the depths of your soul), ask yourself *why*?

Why are you more willing to listen to what someone else thinks about your life, and in essence, YOU, than you are yourself?

I know this feeling a million percent, and if this is a big thing for you, I want to assure you that, as time goes on, you will become more and more confident when it comes to following your own intuition.

This won't stop some people from trying to forewarn you of your impending doom if you dare to take bold steps with your life, but just realise that how they react has way more to do with what they feel is possible for *themselves* than what they see is possible for you.

In 2006, after months of research and after years and years of ignoring the call, I decided once and for all to leave my securely paid corporate job to pursue a new career in teaching.

Shine And Don't Give A Shite

It wasn't that I didn't like my job. The people I worked with were lovely and the company was pretty great, as companies go, and the fact that I met my husband and some of my closest friends while working there says a lot about how much I valued my time there.

The problem was that, deep down, I knew that spending nearly forty hours a week staring at a computer screen was not my true calling.

So, I listened to myself for the first time in a long time and the voice inside told me that I wanted to teach and sing more and write and create. I knew it was true because of the way I felt when I imagined being free to do all of those things, and that sense of freedom felt way more appealing than living my life in a perpetual state of *what if?*

What if I get to the end of my life and regret not going for it?

What if I miss the opportunity to go for it now?

What if I get too fearful and never go for it?

I knew I had to take a big leap to make it come to pass. So I bit the bullet, and after weeks of umm-ing and aghhh-ing, I handed in my resignation and felt an immediate sense of relief.

I knew that I my life was not going to be the same from that moment because I had made a courageous choice and knew more courageous choices would follow, and that excited me massively! Within days I was enrolled into my university course and for the first time in years I felt so invigorated and inspired.

But, as expected, when someone makes the decision to step that far outside of their comfort zone, I had a few people questioning my decision.

What will you do for money?

Aren't you too old to start a new career? (I was 26-and-a-quarter-years-young for goodness sake!)

I'd never do anything that risky!

In the main, I was confident with my decision but when someone questions your sanity, suddenly the doubt-monster sneaks in, pretty friggin' determined to shite all over your show.

All at once these fears came rushing to the surface…

Had I really thought this through?

What if, at 26-and-a-quarter-years-young I, in fact, was too old?

I mean, what the heck was I gonna do for money?

But I had given my decision lots and lots and lots of thought, and before I quit my job, I created a plan.

I would sing in the evenings and teach singing during the day.

I knew that would allow me to make more than enough money to cover my share of our mortgage and bills, plus my university fees. But that very well thought-out plan was ambushed by fearful thoughts of…

…what if I don't make enough money and have to go back to a normal job again?

…what if we decide to start a family in between my degree and I end up half-qualified, having to wait until we are empty-nesters before I have the chance to study again?

…what if by that stage I am well and truly too old to start faffing around with my life?

As you can see, a whole brand new set of *what ifs* were now having a field day in my mind all because I had chosen to let someone else's fears and doubts creep in.

Such is the case when we take big, bold action. Any part of you that's still a bit unsure is totally susceptible to outside influence. It can be easy for others to project their own fears and limitations onto you as you evolve and grow. It may not be intentional, but it can make you doubt yourself.

Of course, that's not to say that it's never good to question your decision or make sure that you have actually considered all options but, often times, when it's coming from a place of fear, it can be enough to totally disregard the confident knowing that you had in the first place.

It can lead you to distrust your inner compass, the part that knows the way and has been guiding you all along.

The key to accessing that inner compass is to STOP listening to what others have to say about your path and START listening to yourself.

If you are tuned into what others think about what you should be doing with your life, you are basically tuned right into *their* fears and doubts and worries *as well as* your own (and then you've got a crap-load of extra fears to deal with).

You have to be brave enough to ignore all the noise and focus 100000% on listening to the whispers of your own soul.

Now, you may be thinking,

Kirsty, that sounds awfully self-centred!

And I assure you that it absolutely *is* self-centred.

It's about feeling back into the <u>centre</u> of <u>yourself.</u>

YOUR INFINITE SELF.

The place where certainty, confidence, excitement, inspiration and magic reside, always. It's about actually trusting yourself, even if no-one else *gets* it.

As I regained my own balance and centred back to myself, I noticed that whenever a fear came up, I would sense a knowing that was way bigger than any doubts that had arisen. A knowing that told me…

Everything is going to be ok. You are supported.

You are on your path. You made the leap.

Now just trust yourself, Kirsty.

And so began my journey of fully learning what that actually means to trust myself, and through the tools I will share with you in this book, you will learn to trust yourself more, too.

You will know that your own inner guidance is the only way forward when it comes to following your calling. No-one else knows you like you do. No-one else can feel what you feel. No-one else has access to your inner knowing but you.

So why look outside for all the answers?

In order to fully SHINE, you need to be prepared to believe in yourself like never before. You also need to know that those intuitive nudges telling you to take a next step are real.

So often we look to others to show us the way instead of remembering that we already have the friggin' map printed inside our souls; we've just gotta be willing to take it out, unfold it and read the damn thing.

That doesn't mean that you're not going to ask others for advice or opinions or feedback. No person is an island.

But it does mean that when you do, you do it for the right reason. If you're seeking guidance because you genuinely want input from others, that's fantastic, but if you're doing it to get their approval, that's a whole different story, and one that won't end well, believe me.

Constantly seeking validation outside of yourself will trap you in an eternal loop of insecurity, self-doubt and frustration. So you have to make a decision to STOP the loop and to START the process of having total faith in yourself.

"Trust in your own wings, in your own Phoenix rising. You have the power to soar so high, from the lowest of depths, if only you trust. You don't need anyone else to approve you, to save you. Just trust in those wings and light up the skies."

Keeley Nicholls

Shine And Don't Give A Shite

Stop Trying to Fix Yourself

…because you're not broken and you never, ever were.

If you feel on any level that you simply cannot be yourself, it is very likely that somewhere in your life you got the message that being you in all your glory was not ok.

Perhaps you made this mean that there was something wrong with you or something about you that needs to be fixed.

Well, I am here to tell you very loudly and clearly that *that* is absolutely horse-shite.

Whether you got that impression from someone you loved and trusted or from magazines, the media or anywhere else, as you do the work within the pages of this book, I really hope that *you* also begin to see just how horse-shitey it is.

Even if not right away, as time goes on and you begin to connect with yourself more deeply, it will become glaringly obvious. But it can be tricky to break away from that belief because so much of our feelings of unworthiness stem from these four words…

I am not enough...

These four words permeate through the minds and hearts of so many of us and they influence the way we feel, behave and what we allow for ourselves.

If you feel that you are not enough, you will not let yourself be fully you. If you feel that you are not enough, you will not share your soul gifts with the world. If you feel you are not enough, you will absolutely not allow yourself to live a magical life.

In whatever way you chalk it up, until you KNOW that you are in fact 1000000000000% ENOUGH and you always have been, you will just keep looking for all the ways that you can finally make yourself enough.

You will be caught in what I call the self-improvement loop. I'm not slating the self-improvement industry (the irony is that this book will probably be categorised as being just that!) but, fundamentally, the term implies that you need to be improved.

That's not to say that you might not benefit from learning new skills or developing existing ones, or even finding ways to improve your life experience BUT if you are doing any of this from a space of not feeling enough, you will only get so far.

The most important thing you can do for yourself is realise that you do not need fixing in any way, shape or form.

The purpose of this book is to help you see that you are already more than enough, and my mission is to help you to know that to be true without a shadow of a doubt.

Stop Buying in to Bogus Beliefs

…because they were never yours to begin with.

I talk a lot about the difference between sabotaging beliefs and supporting beliefs, and in order to shine and not give a shite, you will need to give more attention to your supporting beliefs.

These are the beliefs that are actually going to allow you to show up and be who you really are as opposed to the beliefs that just sabotage you when you attempt to expand and grow. The sabotaging beliefs are, I believe, the main reason why so many people can reach some level of success but then (when it seems like they go past a certain level) everything comes crashing down around them. Our beliefs are always an indicator of what we think is available for us and what we think is not.

If you are not living as you know you could be, then I would hazard a guess that you have at least one humdinger of a sabotaging belief running your show and it will be absolutely limiting your ability to move forward in the way you wish to. You're going to have to get pretty honest about what beliefs are currently running on autopilot and how they are currently affecting your life.

In fact, I would go as far to say that **all** sabotaging beliefs feed into one monstrous belief that is at the very core and, once you address that big belief, things will start to dramatically improve for you.

As I shared earlier *my* monstrous core belief was that I am not good enough, but it had disguised itself for a long time to avoid detection.

It was that belief that had me sabotaging my health and wellbeing when things would start going well for me because I did not believe that I was good enough to experience continued success and happiness.

It's kind of like a runner opting out of a race midway through and blaming it on a twisted ankle, when really she has a core belief that was telling her that she will never win no matter how hard she tries.

It's why someone who has been seeking the love of their life but has a core belief

 that they are not worthy of love always ends relationships a few dates in. To avoid being rejected themselves.

Our beliefs are deep like that. They are like pre-programmed commands that our minds hold onto and then use to direct our entire lives, and it's why the famous Henry Ford quote *(Whether you think you can or whether you think you can't, you're right)* really, really makes sense.

The key is in knowing that you can decide to change that programming at any time.

You just have to be willing to delve into what those beliefs are and perhaps even where they came from. It may not seem like an easy thing to do, but throughout this book I invite you to just notice when a belief pops up.

It may seem like a harmless, perfectly innocuous thought that you have believed for so long that you just kind of dismiss it as nothing. Start to notice how you speak about yourself to others (or to yourself for that matter!) and notice what you believe about yourself and your abilities.

Do you generally believe you <u>can</u> or do you generally believe you <u>can't</u>?

Another important thing to do is seriously question whether the beliefs that you hold are actually *yours*? Or did you inherit the belief now holding you hostage from a parent or loved one or friend or sibling perhaps?

Maybe you grew up hearing that you were lazy. So that became your story and your belief about yourself, and every time you consider doing something that requires effort it pops up to tell you why you simply can't because, you know, *you're just a lazy person and lazy people can't_____.* (fill in the blank)

But now *you* get to believe in the truth of who you really are, not a label that was assigned to you by someone else. You get to believe you are more than the fact that you hated cleaning your room when you were a teenager. You get to see that you are more than the messy bedroom. You are an amazing, magnificent, multi-faceted person capable of and worthy of sooooo much.

What if you started to believe *that* instead? Because whatever story you believe about yourself influences the way you see yourself and what's available and possible for you. So, if you believe that you are lazy how does this limit you? If you see yourself as capable and worthy what becomes available for you?

It's important to understand that our beliefs are formed over time, and as you begin to question and investigate your own, you may go all the way back to an incident or something that happened to you that was the root of the belief. The likelihood is that, somewhere along the line, you adopted a belief and held onto it through re-enforcement from others.

Until you see what your core belief is (and the little baby beliefs that are attached to it) you will keep doing things to sabotage yourself, over and over again. And the worst thing is, you will have no idea why.

But when you start to notice these bogus beliefs that have been hiding in plain sight for most of your life, you'll understand why you have been afraid of shining and sharing your gifts.

And you will finally start to see that your positive belief in yourself will take you anywhere you wanna go.

(Side note: on the subject or beliefs, I would definitely recommend that you check out The Work of Byron Katie. Her website is www.thework.com and it is magical!)

SHINE A LIGHT

What beliefs about yourself have, up until now, really sabotaged you?

Why should I get to have it so easy when there are those who don't?

Why should I get to be so happy when others are suffering?

Why should I get to be so free when others are not?

I always seemed to carry this belief that my feeling good made others feel bad and that it was better just to dim and not be who I was. It was so strange to feel that, but I did none the less.

It was only through doing years and years of inner healing work that I realised that there is nothing wrong with feeling happy any more than there is anything wrong with feeling sad. Feelings are just feelings. They are meant to be felt and expressed.

I tried to suppress my joy for a long time because I would allow the times I was told I was *too happy* to seep into my consciousness, creating the false belief that it was more admirable to be sad. But how could me containing my joy ever be a good thing for me or anyone else?

If you are suppressing your joy, you are suppressing all of that which lights you up, which is such as shame.

The truth is, if you are a naturally happy, joyful person, you have every right to live from that space and allow that energy to radiate outwards without apology.

Believe me, you being you and living life from that place of authentic joy will, by extension, have a positive impact on those around you as well as the whole planet, so keep radiating it and never, ever contain it.

"Keep going. Show your joys, your passions, your beauty. You are so needed here. You are essential to all that is going on."

Debbie McDermott

Shine And Don't Give A Shite

Stop Fighting For Your Limitations

…because there is soooooooo much possibility within you.

Have you ever found yourself in this kind of convo?

Ernie: *Oh wow, I really love your artwork! You really have such an amazing talent for colour blending. Seriously, you're awesome! Have you considered selling your pieces?*

Bert: *Oh nooooo, me? I'm nowhere near as good as I should be after all the years I've been painting. I spend way too much time faffing around and it takes me ages to finish just one. I should be quicker. Nobody would buy anyway. Besides, even if I wanted to sell them, I have no idea how to market myself. I'm rubbish with technology.*

Ernie: *Oh, I can help you with that if you like? That's one of my passions and I'm a really good teacher. I'd be happy to help.*

Bert: *No, that would be a waste of your time. I never pick things up, even if I have a great teacher. Selling my art has been a dream of mine for years but I should just be realistic. Thanks anyway…*

Well, maybe you're not an artist but has anyone ever complimented you in an area that you are actually quite passionate about but instead of receiving the compliment you have found yourself fighting for your limitations?

Maybe you have been the one offering the compliment and the other person has literally told you all the reasons why (despite clearly having heaps of talent for something) they actually suck.

They have literally fought for their limitations because they feel that they *are* their limitations. The truth is, when we are faced with the potential of growth, transformation and change, it can be really, really horrifying to the part of us that believes that it is limited (I refer to this part of us as The Limited Self).

The Limited Self has a very limited perspective of the world and as such, it inhibits your ability to grow and evolve because it knows only what it has experienced up until now, nothing beyond that. It does not know that it is, in fact, infinite.

It's main pre-occupation, therefore, is in keeping you safe and alive by staying within those limits, where it knows it is safe.

This includes avoiding anything that feels like death to it and death to The Limited Self is literally **anything** that takes you beyond what it has experienced before.

That is why, when you are just about to take a big leap in life, you may find yourself overcome with self-doubt, clammy hands and a monologue entitled: **ALL THE REASONS WHY I SHOULDN'T DO THIS** on repeat at one thousand decibels in your brain.

Of course these kinds of warning signs are totally appropriate, helpful and potentially life-saving when you are about to leap, let's say, into the path of an oncoming vehicle because you're too busy texting your mate about where you're meant to be meeting for coffee.

That's what Your Limited Self is there for. It remembers seeing or even experiencing the real danger of being hit by a car and its mission is to keep you safe from that. It will scream: *Look the eff up, you are in serious danger, girl!* in its best Whoopi G voice when you are *actually* in serious danger.

Theories abound that this part of our brains was totally on high alert when we were dwelling in caves and had the real and regular peril of being eaten by a lion, tiger or bear, but as most people are, hopefully, no longer faced with the threat of being eaten alive on a regular basis, it now sees peril in anything that could be perceived as even a little bit scary to you.

Things that take you beyond who you have been and into a new territory of expansion; a place that The Limited Self has no concept of or has a previous *bad* experience of in the past.

Now, I'm no anthropologist but I know from personal experience how true this is. I only have to slightly think about stepping a pinky-toe out of my comfort zone and my nervous system will respond as if I am about to skydive from the topmost tip of Kilimanjaro. This is because The Limited Self will respond, not only to legitimately terrifying scenarios (for which we really do need it) but also anything that, deep within, you have a trauma around or a deep fear of (even if you don't know it's there) .

It will be on high alert to anything that may re-trigger that fear or past trauma, even if it's something that seems pretty normal to you. It also explains why you may find yourself sabotaging your happiness or success then feeling frustrated because you can't understand why.

The likelihood is that you have a fear attached to moving beyond where you currently are. Perhaps it's the fear of the unknown, but it can also be triggered by a conscious or unconscious past experience that Your Limited Self now associates with pain or danger.

I'll give you an example of how this presents itself in my life. I have a big fear of heights. I get all kinds of weird, nervy feelings in my belly if I am on the edge of somewhere high up (even some ladders). I'm also really afraid of falling and I think this relates to a trauma I suffered as a toddler when I fell down the stairs and pretty much died, and even though I don't consciously remember the experience, it would explain the fear I still have.

I have told myself for years that I could never, ever, ever be someone who was brave enough to do something like skydiving. I mean, that is literally two of my biggest fears rolled into one terrifying pursuit. So, with this in mind, of course My Limited Self would be making itself very known if I did actually decide to (in a rush of bravery) skydive from the top of Kilimanjaro.

It would be shaking my whole nervous system to the core as if to say: *Don't you remember what happened? Don't do it. Don't do it. For all that is good and holy, DON'T DO IT, Kirsty, you fool.*

And on and on and on it would go, desperately trying to get my attention because it is tasked with keeping me alive.

That's how amazing and loyal The Limited Self is.

But let's just say that my motivation for doing the skydive is to actually face my fear and to move through it. Imagine I'd thought about it for some time, knew that the odds of actually being hurt were slim and was willing to take that risk because I no longer want to be scared of doing it. I want to experience the exhilaration and the rush and the freedom.

The thing is, My Limited Self does not get *any* of this. It can only stay faithful to its job of protecting me from the limited perspective it has -- one that involves crashing to my death.

A bit like a well-meaning (but very over protective) parent who constantly reminds their child about the time they tripped over the coffee table when they were learning to walk and therefore should not take the risk of daring to (heaven forbid) run.

But at some stage the child must decide for themselves whether running is actually a risk. Yes, they could fall again and yes, they could be injured. It's logical that staying within their comfort zone of walking would be safer, but just imagine how much freedom and possibility and expansion would be available once they learn to run!

So the child must choose between staying in the limits of the slow meander or the thrill of the sprint.

And if I could place my cash on it, I would bet every time that the majority of children will choose the latter.

This is because young children have not yet learned to listen to limitations. They tend to follow their inner guidance to a tee! And if they chose to run, they have to actually see themselves as a runner and no longer identify with the limited perspective of their over protective parent.

This may seem like a silly analogy, but I share it because, like the child, you too must decide whether you wish to move past the limitations that have kept you stuck by no longer identifying with them. Only then will you be able to experience the freedom and possibility and expansion that lays in wait for you outside of your comfort zone.

If I wanted to no longer identify as someone who is afraid of heights, I would have to first decide to stop fighting for what I previously saw as a limitation for myself. And instead see myself as someone who can absolutely skydive or do anything that I have been, up until now, terrified of doing.

At the moment you might feel really limited in your own ways or feel that you just don't have the capability to be, do, have and experience all that is meant for you. So, instead of seeing beyond this, it's easier to stay focused on your limitations and to fight for them.

But when you actively fight for your limitations, you're saying: *I don't want to change. Change is too hard.* And whilst staying the same may seem like the safer option, it's also the most soul-destroying option.

If you want to truly be free, the first step is choosing to awaken to and remember who you really are.

Only then will you start to see these limitations for the illusions they really are, and you will stop fighting to defend them.

Once you stop fighting for your limitations, you create a space for your infinite, limitless potential; for what is possible for you beyond fear and beyond the narrow perspective of Your Limited Self (or anyone else's Limited Self, for that matter).

The Limited Self has a story about how things *should* be based on your past experiences, so as you move beyond it you change the story. You change what it now sees is possible for you.

But for a while there Your Limited Self will try to sabotage you.It will stay attached to what it knows and remind you why you can't move past that. But as you grow and evolve and transcend your fears you will identify less with The Limited Self and start to live from Your Infinite Divine Self.

Though, bear in mind: it's so important to respect and honour Your Limited Self for what it has done and what it will continue to do for you, which is keeping you safe and alive. Be grateful for that, but remember, you can make it clear that you are excited to change, that change is good! Sooner or later it will be on-board and you will find yourself accomplishing previously terrifying pursuits with ease.

But just as it must, as you grow and evolve and push past your previous limitations, it will pop up to put the fear of God into you once more as you reach new limits.

Your job is to just keep remembering that it is there to keep you safe, and if there is no real life or death situation it's fine to trust your deeper inner guidance and move forward.

You may notice this shift occurring as you move through this book. Just when you thought you'd literally healed everything you will be slapped across the forehead with a limiting belief or fear that you never knew existed!

Sorry to be the bearer of bad news but this will keep occurring because you are here to keep expanding and with expansion comes new limits. But rest assured, it gets easier the more connected to yourself you allow yourself to be.

Also, as you move through this book you may notice feelings of resistance that come up, either in response to an exercise or even just an abstract idea that you are hearing for the first time. If Your Limited Self feels threatened by this new information or it triggers a deeper fear, just acknowledge it. Just sit with all the sensations that come up (and there may be lots!) but know that you are not The Limited Self and you never have been. Throughout this book I will keep reminding you that you are in fact very far from limited and what you are feeling are impermanent emotions, habits, patterns, beliefs and fears that will sooner or later pass you by.

I don't expect you just to take my word for it, though. As you learn to connect more and more with Your Infinite Divine Self and release more and more of what has been causing you to feel limited, you will know just how magical you truly are. Your only job is to start focusing more on your magic and less on your limitations -- and definitely STOP fighting for them!

SHINE A LIGHT

How have you been fighting for your limitations?

"There are NO limits in anyone's potential. Every single person is here for a reason and has a purpose, and you may not know what that is now, and that's perfectly ok but you ARE here for something great."

Jessica Jones

(aka: The Fat Funny One)

Stop Trying to Please Everyone

…because it's an impossible task.

I once saw a meme that made me laugh. Something along the lines of: *You can't please everyone, you're not Nutella!*

(For those of you who don't know what Nutella is, it's a heavenly, rich, sweet, chocolate spread, plus, where the hell have you been?!)

The meme really made me smile, not only because it was funny but, because there's a HUGE truth in it: **you really** *can't* please everyone, no matter what you do.

The simple fact is, sometimes people won't like you, no matter how amiable and nice and Nutellery-sweet you are. This is a really important thing to grasp, especially if you feel you are very much a people-pleaser.

When I first started doing this work and when I'd feel inspired to create something like a blog post or record video, or even write something, I'd instantly find myself watering down my idea in order to make it as palatable (aka: sweet) as possible.

Shine And Don't Give A Shite

So, just like the jar of Nutella, I could please as many people as possible. I would allow my desire to be liked and accepted to overshadow my truth.

All the while I'd be thinking: *How can I make sure that I'm staying away from ANYTHING that may go against the grain? Maybe I should avoid saying 'xyz' incase people think it's too much. What if people hate what I have created or disagree with my truth?*

My need for validation and acceptance was exhausting and quite honestly, it was a major snooze-fest.

I really didn't know it, but my life had been built on being the most likeable me I could be, and to be seen in any light other than *nice* and *accommodating* and *agreeable* was like death to me.

But in trying to be all of those things to everyone, I was diminishing my truth, my fire, my magic, my light and myself. I was afraid of what would happen if I actually let myself be fully me, without watering down my truth or hiding what I truly wanted to say, without apologising for the fire in my belly, AND without giving a rat's arse about what anyone thought about it to boot!

I share this because, if you are reading this, recognising yourself in my story, you may be thinking: *Well, awesome for you, Kirsty, but how do I stop giving a rat's arse about what others think of me?* I want to assure you it is possible. It will take **deciding** to be someone who values and likes themselves *above* any need to be liked by all of the people all of the time.

And by realising that being liked by all of the people all of the time is an impossible standard.

It's ok that you are not Nutella.

It's ok to be Marmite (for the record, I bloody LOVE it).

It's ok for some people to love you and some people to be indifferent about you and for some people to really dislike you.

You have to decide to let go of the illusion that what others think of you in any way reflects who you are and what you are worthy of.

Once you approve of and like and validate yourself your whole life will change.

When you simply accept that a part of you has been seeking validation, approval and acceptance from outside of yourself, you start the process of letting it go. Then and only then will you actually be able to be fully you and live your magical life, without a second thought to what your next door neighbour's cousin, Nigel, thinks about you…

…coz, quite frankly, what Nigel thinks about you is none of your damn business.

SHINE A LIGHT

How is your need for approval and validation holding you back from being totally true to yourself?

"You are not for everybody. Some people will be offended by your happiness. Turned off by your sadness. Envious of your growth. Cynical about your success. But the one thing you cannot do, in spite of those people, is STOP being you."

Natasha K Benjamin

Stop Shrinking

…because you playing small serves no-one.

I really dislike the sayings: *don't get too big for your boots* or *you'll get a big head* or *stop blowing your own trumpet* and other silly phrases that look to shame those who celebrate themselves.

Picture the scene...

You have just completed something AWESOME.

Perhaps you landed the new job you've been praying for. Maybe you just passed a milestone exam. Or you got healthy and lost the weight that you'd been trying to lose for some time.

You feel proud of yourself. Really, really proud. You know you've grown in massive confidence along the way. You share the news excitedly with your friends and family and colleagues, and whilst most people are sooooo genuinely happy for you, there's that ONE comment that sets out to deflate all of that self-confidence and pride in one spiteful, gut-wrenching blow.

The snide remark that, although disguised as a bit of fun, is really meant to bring you down a peg or two. *The ooh look at you Miss High and Mighty...aren't you pleased with yourself?!** (*or something similarly mean-spirited)

It STINKS and it STINGS. Like hell.

Worst of all, it triggers a soul-destroying spiral of shaming you into silence.

For a second there, you actually believed that you had EVERY SINGLE RIGHT in the world to pat yourself on the back, big yourself up, feel pretty darn good about yourself and your life.

But now you feel like the biggest show-off ever for daring to throw your accomplishments in the face of others in such a *braggy* way. You start thinking: *Who on EARTH do I think I am? I'm nothing special. Why did I have to go showing off like that?*

You learn from the experience that it's wrong to grow, it's wrong to celebrate yourself, it's wrong to expand, it's wrong to get too big, and it's wrong to share your triumphs.

So, instead, you SHRINK.

You learn that it's safer to play small and to shy away from your greatness, pushing it down inside of you, deflecting compliments along the way so as not to invite any attention that could be misconstrued as vanity.

But the insecurity that you feel actually was never yours to begin with. It was theirs. And you **do not** have to carry it.

You **do not** have to shrink when others try to shame you for being big, bold, brave or beautiful, and if someone else happens to be triggered by your expansion or your light, it is 100000% *their* stuff. The truth is, when you choose to live your life from a place of intention rather than limitation, you'll trigger some people.

If you choose to quit your job, sell your house and do absolutely nothing for 12 months, you'll trigger some people.

If you choose to pursue your life-long dream of acting on Broadway, you'll trigger some people.

If you choose to stay single instead of settling down and getting hitched, you'll trigger some people.

If you choose to have children and still be really happy and successful in the work you love, you'll trigger some people.

If you choose to not to have children and spend all your money on whatever the hell you like, you'll trigger some people.

If you are strong and know what feels right for you in your life and you follow that without justifying or apologising or explaining to others, **you'll trigger some people.**

When someone has believed all their life that they are limited and you go ahead and choose to move past *their* perceived limitations, YOU WILL TRIGGER THEM. There will be those who see their trigger as an opportunity to grow and those who will see it as a reason to make you feel bad for living your life in a way they think they never could.

Shine And Don't Give A Shite

Either way, it is absolutely **not** your responsibility to keep yourself small and squished into a box just so your best friend, sister or colleague gets to stay comfortable.

You being fully you, in all your magnificence, does not steal anyone else's chance to be fully *them* in all their glory! You do not owe your light to anyone, and every time you shrink you are buying into the illusion that there is some kind of limit on how happy, successful or lit-up someone can possibly be!

But you'll soon awaken to the fact that there is no limit.

By continuing to expand, no matter what, you set an example of what is possible for others if they too choose to look beyond their perceived limitations

Because, really, there *is* no point at which you need to stop and say: *Oh well, I've done too well for myself so I should really call it a day now...*

Or: *It's really not fair that I get to be this happy or beautiful or free, I need to dull down a bit now...*

Or: *I have really had way too much Ben & Jerry Phish Food ice cream; I really must share it with Enrico before it all runs out...* (ok, that one might apply)

That was the thing that I found so hard to finally let go of. No, not my insatiable love of chocolate ice cream, but the twisted belief that, somehow, me being me, shining my light, sharing my gifts and living a totally lit-up life was somehow greedy and selfish and wrong and made me a terrible person.

So I started to hold back from sharing and celebrating things that were going well for me, because I didn't want to be *that* person (you know, the one who is seen as being too much).

So I learned to shrink because it felt easier that way.

And I'm hazarding a guess that if you are this far into this book, you too have found yourself shrinking in order to be accepted or because of a fear that you'll be rejected or abandoned somehow.

And yes, there *is* a real chance some people won't like you anymore or they might reject you as you choose to be fully you and no longer shrink yourself, but I'd say: *so what if they do?*

In the big scheme of things, are those really valid enough reasons to NOT BE WHO YOU ARE? Is anyone who is not willing to support you in being **you** really be someone you'd want in your corner anyway? Don't you deserve more?

Of course you bloody do!

When you really break it down to that simple truth that you deserve to be accepted for who you are, you'll see that you keeping yourself small and limited in order to keep somebody else happy is a completely messed up way of living your life.

Otherwise, you will be living your life for others and being someone you think will be the most acceptable and loveable and likeable version of you, and that will suck.

BIG TIME.

I had that realisation the day I found myself asking myself: *Kirsty, are you really going to hold yourself back from living the life that you're here to live and being who you truly are just so that others get to feel comfortable?*

That was the question I really had to sit with for a long time. I had to ask myself if I was willing to hide myself and keep myself stuck and small just because there's a part of me that was scared that I was going to trigger somebody else? Over the years of doing this deeper inner work, I began to realise that, as much as I thought it was kind and compassionate, and perhaps even admirable to shrink, keeping others from feeling their own shit was not helping them at all. It was time for me to start being me, come hell or high water.

But it took me what seemed like an eternity to see all the ways I was holding myself back because I felt that those I loved would reject me for being too much, but in the end, I had to choose—between *my* happiness and someone else's.

The thing is, for some people, this would be a total non-issue. They might revel in the prospect of *outdoing* those they care about and may even see it as healthy competition, but for those of us who are sensitive souls, the ones who can empathically feel what others are feeling all the live long day, we can also feel how triggers affect them. We can feel the insecurities rising within them when they find out someone has bought a bigger house than them or made a bolder choice.

It triggers the part of them that believes their worth is determined by how well *they* are doing in relation to others.

They're also still believing in the lie that life is about what you accomplish and *what you have* rather than *who you are*.

The truth is that when you give yourself permission to expand into the fullness of who you are, you are going to piss some people off, but guess what?

It is NOT your responsibility to protect them.

When you stop worrying about what others will feel and just live your life, you actually create a space where they can see where they might be hiding from *their* own greatness. It gives them a chance to heal and release whatever is causing them to feel the way they feel about you shining and, in effect, helps them to become a truer them.

Honestly, do you want to spend your life worrying about what other people think of you or do you want to be free?

The bottom line is, some people will give you crap when you decide to go beyond the limits of what they perceived was possible for you (or them). They may demand that you explain and justify yourself or they may try to make you feel small for daring to be all that you are, but please, please, please, don't ever shrink yourself to fit someone else's limited view of you.

Remember that you shining your brilliant light will only trigger those who deep down know they are hiding their own light. So, celebrate that, because you are showing them what's possible when someone becomes reacquainted with their inner spark, and you never know how much that might inspire them.

Shine And Don't Give A Shite

"If you stay the real you, the truest you, the deepest you, the most alive you, you might trigger someone and eventually help them to release their shit.

Otherwise you can stay small, while enabling others to stay small and you can feel codependent on each other while completely sacrificing true fulfillment and freedom."

Kyle Cease

(Transformational Comedian, Speaker and New York Times Best-Selling Author)

Stop Listening to the Should-ers

…because life has no blueprint.

My six-year old daughter Liberty has this incredible book called *Good Night Stories for Rebel Girls* and we both love it. Each two-page spread tells the story of a real life (past or present) female who is considered heroic and somewhat rebellious in their pursuit of being true to themselves.

From the freedom fighter, Harriet Tubman, to the scientist, Marie Curie, to the painter, Frida Kahlo, the book is filled from cover to cover with the most inspiring and illuminating stories of those who stood up against the narrative of *should* and chose a path of *possibility*.

Libby and I read each mini biography and explore each accompanying portrait awe-inspired at the courage it took for each of the women to stand in their truth and to go against the norm. Being a bit of an inner rebel myself, I honestly feel such pride when reading what some women had to overcome in order to create change and impact in the world.

*Favilli, E and Cavallo, F. (2017). Good Night Stories for Rebel Girls

Shine And Don't Give A Shite

One such is the story of the Mexican-born, Eufrosina Cruz, who, after being told by her father that women were only good for making tortillas and children, soon showed him how much of a big old pile of steaming poo that was.

She left home, funded her own studies by selling chewing gum and fruit on the street, and returned home with a job as a teacher. She also founded an organization called QUIEGO to help women build their own lives.

Oh, and she later became the first indigenous woman to be elected president of the state congress. I mean, how amazing!

Reading Eufrosina's story made me realise how utterly devastating it would be if literally everyone listened to the *should-ers* of the world. The people who want to box you in and tell you what and where you should be in your life right about now rather than support you in *your* choices.

As much as her father may have felt well-meaning and justified in telling Eufrosina that she could not be more than a mother and tortilla maker, he was coming from a totally limited place.

A place where he could not see beyond what could be possible for his amazing daughter other than what he believed was possible for women. The mantra of *that* place is…

this is how life should be.

Those who follow that mantra believe that life has a particular blueprint, determined by your gender, age, culture, religion, skin colour, family or your lineage.

How depressing and bleak it would be if we all lived life that way? If we let those six words be our mantra for life? If we actually believed that it was true?

When I finally decided to stop living my life on autopilot and start living from my own intuition, I encountered A LOT of *should-ing* from those who thought I ought to be living life differently.

The thing is, this is quite normal to encounter as you start to break free from the norms of life. We have (in many ways) been conditioned to believe that life is meant to be a succession of boxes to be ticked off one by one. Our seemingly only gauge to indicate if we are doing things the *right* way.

But there *is* no specific way that your life should go.

Deep down, I have always known this to be true. That there is no blueprint for mine or anyone else's life and this has become even more apparent to me the further along my path I have travelled.

I know that every single one of us is here to live a totally unique life, and it takes being courageous enough to follow the beat of your own drum to live it.

I mean, just imagine if you lived your whole life from a place of what you felt you *should* be doing? How boring and predictable would life be?

When instead it can be an epic adventure. Of course with twists and turns, but one where you get to be freely you and follow your own unique path.

Shine And Don't Give A Shite

There will be those who read that and argue: *so you're saying that it would be ok if we all just stopped paying bills, and stopped being a law-abiding citizens and stopped looking out for others? So it's ok if people just wanna be mean to others and rob banks and sell drugs if that's what they feel like doing?*

(Yes, I've seriously had someone say this to me *insert eye-roll*)

But, it's only the limited, fearful part of us that would believe being free would equate to being a selfish arse.

It's also why so many people won't allow themselves to even consider what life could be like beyond the limitations they have placed on themselves. Because deep down we all know that if we were all tuned into who we truly are, there would be MORE love on the planet, MORE light, MORE creativity, MORE joy, MORE connection, MORE peace and MORE service to others.

You just have to look at the lives of those like Nelson Mandela, John Lennon and Fred Rogers to see how true that is.

To see what a profound effect someone can have on the planet when they don't operate from that limited space of *should* but come from a space of *possibility.*

Those who are creating (and have created) the most positive impact in the world have always been those who have gone against the grain instead of listening to what society told them they *ought* to be doing. They live and create and experience life from a place of **infinite** possibility instead of **finite** should.

If you don't believe me, just start with YOU allowing yourself to be more freely YOU and see the magic that ripples from your life into the world.

The part of you that wants to believe that this is all just airy-fairy-mumbo-jumbo-nonsense is the part of you that has always felt it needed to stay limited and in a box to be safe. The more you allow yourself to look beyond this, the more you will know the truth of this. Don't take my word for it. Just make the decision to stop listening to the *should-ers* and reconnect back with who you truly are.

No-one else on this planet will ever walk in your shoes, and as much as from the outside some may think they need to remind you how you should be living your life, it is only because they have forgotten their own way.

That's usually why many *should* on others in the first place. They have not yet found within themselves the courage to break away from their own sense of limitation, and your desire to be free from the norm massively pisses them off. They bought into the lie that said *this is how life should be* and now they are trying to push that rulebook it onto you instead of letting themselves be free also! And the voice that tells them *this is how life should be* has kept them playing small with their lives and their gifts is not the voice that will inspire you. So stop listening!

Only then will you discover that it is through connecting with Your Infinite Divine Self and tuning into the gifts that you are here to share with the world that you will become inspired and will be an inspiration for others. Just you wait and see.

Shine And Don't Give A Shite

"Can you remember who you were before the world told you who you should be?"

Charles Bukowski

Stop Worrying About Being Judged

…because it's only how you're judging yourself that matters.

More than anything, the fear of being judged can hold someone back from truly being themselves.

Maybe you are scared of being judged for being too much, too successful, too big for your boots, too happy, too unrealistic, too woo-woo, too strange, too abundant, too spiritual, too confident, too clever, too liked, too creative, too lazy, too powerful, too eccentric, too bold, too much for others to bear, too bright, too random, too weird, too wired, too showy, too bubbly, too childish, too off the walls, too out there, too big headed, too confident, too sure of yourself, too optimistic, too radical, too trusting, too open, too free, too unconventional, too introverted, too extroverted, too quiet, too loud…too WHAT-THE-HECK-EVER!

The thing is, as you can see, someone could literally judge you for **any** reason, and unless you are willing to keep hiding who you really are, nothing you can do will change that (even then, I bet they would find another reason to judge you, so you can never win!)

Shine And Don't Give A Shite

Assuming that you are doing nothing immoral or illegal, or hurting anyone in the process, how anyone else feels about you living your life and being true to yourself is irrelevant.

If they want to judge you for being true to yourself, so what? Let them judge. It's *their* wasted energy.

It only becomes *your* wasted energy if you allow their judgements (or perceived judgements) to define you or stop you from being who you really are.

Although, let's be honest, if you're focusing on how much others are judging you for being *too* anything, it is likely that you also have very similar judgements about yourself.

Now, I know those words are like nails up a chalkboard to someone who is convinced that *once everyone else stops judging them they will be free to live their life.*

The harsh truth is, deep down you are your own biggest doubter. You are our own worst critic and, quite frankly, YOU are the only one holding yourself back from being you and living your life.

Yes, I said it. I know it stings like a biatch, but it *is* only the thoughts and feelings within *you* that will dictate whether or not you are going to allow the things in life that you desire, not the thoughts and feelings of those around you.

That's not to say that how you feel about yourself has not been influenced by outside messaging because it's very likely that it has, but right now you get to decide how you feel about you.

You really do not need anyone else's permission, support or validation to be YOU. You just get to decide that anything less than that is not an option.

Being true to yourself often has little to do with other people.

At first it can feel that way because we create layers to protect who we truly are if we have been hurt, traumatised or believe that being who we are will lead to judgements.

I know for damn sure that it can be really hard to step out and be who we truly are and I totally acknowledge that, as everybody has had totally different life experiences, it may be much harder for some than others.

It may not be easy, but once you step back into Your Divine Essence you will see that...

Other people's opinions of you are not keeping you small.

Other people's opinions of you are not keeping you stuck.

Other people's opinions of you are not keeping you from being who you are.

It's how *you* feel about you that matters, and you get to change how you feel about yourself by remembering and honouring who you truly are beyond the self-judgement.

Once you are totally, fully and securely ok with you, it will not matter one iota what anyone else thinks. You will know that you're good with you, and that is all that really matters when it comes to fully allowing yourself to be who you are.

"When you no longer need approval from others like the air you breathe, the possibilities in life are endless. What an interesting little prison we build from the invisible bricks of other people's opinions."

Jacob Nordby

Stop Hiding Your Brilliant Light

…because the world needs it more than you know.

Whenever I enter a new situation, whether it's a job, friendship or social circle, one of the last things I tend to share with people is the fact that I can sing.

I remember when I was completing my teaching training and my mentor at the time discovered that I was a singer, he arranged for myself and a colleague to perform an acoustic version of Journey's classic song *Don't Stop Believing* in front of the whole school!

Now, to give some background, by that stage I had already been singing professionally at different events and in various venues for about six years, so the actual singing part came easily. What did not come so easily to me was actually sharing my gift in a totally different environment than the darkened venues I had been used to. I have always been shy and relatively quiet in new situations, so deciding to put myself in front of audiences each week and perform for a living was a somewhat paradoxical challenge.

Shine And Don't Give A Shite

I mean, surely you only choose that kind of work if you love being in the limelight and love being applauded, right? But honestly, both made me cringe no matter how many times I stood on a stage.

My singing work had really evolved over time. From initially being in a band where I was surrounded by four very experienced musicians to being in duos where I always had someone at my side.

When I eventually decided to go solo I became sooooo much more aware of how the performance side of singing does not come naturally to me. The awkwardness of not knowing what to say in between tracks or how to shimmy on stage or engage with the audience were always (and still are) things that make me cringe! But the actual singing? That has always felt like pure ease to me. I LOVE SINGING. I sing everywhere. I make up songs about whatever I am doing in that moment, and I know all the words to pretty much every Whitney song ever recorded.

Yet, the thought of singing in front of hundreds of the children who I had been teaching as *just* Mrs. Caló for months mortified me! Not just because children can be the harshest critics, but because I had a feeling that in sharing this part of myself outside of the typical music environments put me waaaaaay outta my comfort zone! Nevertheless, I plucked up the courage and somewhere between Maths and phonics, myself and the other Year 3 teacher, Gerard, who was stunning on guitar, brought the house down with our rendition of the Journey classic.

The kids and teachers LOVED it!

My musical partner had already been known to pull out his guitar and start jamming in front of his class, and I really admired how he just owned his talent, fully. He was used to sharing all of his gifts with his class.

However, for me, there had been this hold back—a part of me not wanting to SHINE too brightly or be seen or be...judged. I mean, I was there to *teach*, not sing. There was something comforting about being able to compartmentalise my skills like that. Don't ask me why.

A few years later, I was teaching in another school and our class was to sing in a multi-school musical event. Each week a singing teacher would come in and run a rehearsal for us so that we could learn the songs we'd be performing on the day.

Overhearing me singing along with the kids, out of the blue, she excitedly asked if I would be willing to sing solo in front of the hundreds of children, siblings, parents, grandparents and friends attending the concert. No big deal, you know.

OH. MY. GOD. What would people think? What if I looked like an idiot? What if all the parents thought I was a bit of a tit?

Part of me wanted to politely decline, but my entire class (having heard the on-the-spot request) all erupted into a chant: *Do it, do it, do it. Oh please, Mrs. Caló, will you do it? PLEASE?*

Only a Miss Trunchbull-level heartless hag of a teacher could shrug off those adorable words of encouragement. I knew I had to do it or I would never hear the end of it!

So, fast forward a few weeks and there I was, standing in front of 500 or so people in a glaringly lit auditorium singing Katrina and The Waves' anthem *Walking on Sunshine* at the top of my lungs, and all I could hear were the cheers and woops of not only my class but the hundreds of other children behind me.

In that moment, as I took in the kids' delightful cheers encouraging me to give it all I had, I realised how utterly ridiculous I had been to be afraid of sharing my gift.

After the show, the grandmother of a girl in my class came up to me and, with a wide smile, told me how much she had enjoyed my song. She said she had no idea that I could sing like that, and then she said something to me which, even to this day, brings a tear to my eye. She leaned in and whispered:

...don't hide your light under a bushel, Mrs. Caló!

...and with a wink of her eye, off she went.

That quick exchange has been with me since then because she was right. There really was no need to hide my gifts, and there is absolutely no reason for you to hide yours.

Maybe, like me, you feel that completely owning all of your incredible talents will be met with judgement or criticism, and that is what stops you.

Maybe you don't want to be too much or you worry that people will just think you're *showing off* if you do all those things that come so easily and effortlessly to you. But those things come so easily and effortlessly to you only *because* they are your natural talents, and there is no need to apologise or feel in any way that it's wrong to own them.

Imagine if the likes of David Bowie, Bruce Lee or Maya Angelou had all worried so much about what others thought of them, that they never shared their gifts with the world?

At some stage they all had to abandon any sense of giving a shite and get the hell on with being who they were born to be!

The bottom line is this:

When you care too much about what others will think of you, you don't get to be who you truly are or share the gifts you are here to share.

You don't write the book. You don't create the masterpiece. You don't share your art. You don't beatbox. You don't help others. You don't sing. You don't dance. You don't live fully. You don't share any of the incredible things that make you so completely you, and that is such a shame.

You were born with a unique blend of soul gifts that only YOU possess, and it really is time to start sharing them with the world. Like, yesterday.

So, no more hiding *your* light under a bushel, you hear?!

"Stop being afraid of really OWNING your worth. Stop being afraid of your own power, your potential, your growth, and start RESPECTING yourself enough to shine your light FOR REALS."

Hannah Mang

Stop Worrying About Outshining Others

…because the sun does not give a shite about blinding you.

One of the things that really holds us back can be not wanting to outshine someone close to us. It could be that you already know exactly who that person is, or it could be that you really don't have a clue.

I would bet money that we all, at some stage throughout our journey, will hold ourselves back a bit so as not to make someone else feel bad or inadequate.

When you think about being your brightest, boldest, most beautiful self, do you get an intuitive sense that someone in particular (or maybe more than one person) may feel jealous or envious? It could just be that it's a fear, but even having such a fear can really make you dim your light.

Take a moment to close your eyes and, in your mind's eye, see yourself living your whole truth and nothing but your truth.

What are you wearing? How do you look and feel in your body? How are you spending your days? How is your life totally lit up?

Shine And Don't Give A Shite

See it all and feel that version of yourself NOW (not sometime in the future). Really allow the energy of your light to well up inside you, then ask yourself: *who might be in resistance to this, and why?*

Let your intuition speak to you. Take some time now to pause and reflect on this. (Remember though, it does not mean that what comes up is definitely true, but if it comes up, it means that, on some level, you have made this true to you.)

It could be that a part of you is really afraid that all of your friends will hate you and your family will disown you if you suddenly start living your dreams. The likelihood of all that happening is pretty slim, even if you have the most awful people in your life, but fears are fears, and it's important to consider how they may be holding you back.

Let's say that upon doing this exercise, you identify that your sister (let's call her Gemma) would be in huge resistance to you being your true, authentic self.

In fact, whilst you were visualising being your badass self and living your bestest, most expansive life, her face popped in your mind and she was very jealous. You could feel that jealousy in your body and it took over the feeling of excitement that you had been dwelling in moments before.

Gemma means the world to you and you would hate for her to be jealous of you. It reminds you of when you were young and your mum would praise your excellent school work, and you sensed this made Gemma feel less than.

You, always wanting to protect her feelings, would go out of your way to highlight all the amazing things that Gemma had been doing too, so that she didn't feel left out. Now, through doing this exercise, you have an awareness that your relationship with your sister is so important to you, as is protecting her feelings.

You are now aware of all the times you have shied away from celebrating things that have been going well for you when Gemma is around, and the more you think of it, you have actually turned down opportunities to do things that you know she would love because, again, you don't want to her to feel left in your shadow. You would much rather just stay at the same level so that she never feels left behind…and on and on and on it goes.

Now, of course this is a totally made up scenario (unless you really do have a sis called Gemma who you are doing your utmost to wrap up in a cotton wall for fear of her facing her own stuff) but you might have your own version of events going on inside your own mind.

Yet, the truth is, if you limit yourself because you fear you will outshine others, you are actually believing that they are not able to shine too! Which is totally untrue because we were all born to SHINE in our own unique ways, and you shining does not rob anyone else of *their* chance to shine. Remember that next time you are tempted to dim your light.

SHINE A LIGHT

Who are you worried about outshining?

Shine And Don't Give A Shite

"Don't dim your light to accommodate someone else's smallness. We are all born to shine big and bright.

Rebecca Campbell

Stop Distracting Yourself from Yourself

…because you are what you have been searching for.

My Divine Wake-Up Call had actually been brewing under the surface for years. It was brought to a head once I had become a mum, and this newborn bundle of love, light and awesomeness we named Liberty changed my life forever. The years before Libby was born were all leading me to fully awakening to who I truly was and what the hell I was actually here to do in the world.

When I was in my final year at senior school I remember visiting the local university and instantly knew that I wanted to study to become a teacher. I remember reading the prospectus and imaging myself receiving the A-level grades that were required in order for me to apply.

Fast forward to Summer 1997 and, although I had received the grades I needed, I didn't have the money to apply for university. The government had recently withdrawn the student grants that would have allowed students in my year group to go to university fully-funded, and there was no way I was going to put any pressure on my parents to pay for a three-year stint at uni.

Shine And Don't Give A Shite

So instead, I decided to keep working my two part-time jobs -- pulling pints in a cool musical bar by night and serving fry-ups in a coffee shop by day. I thought I would be better off having a few years study-free so that I could save enough money to apply for my course a few years down the line.

But time slipped by. I got so used to working and making money (which I would blow on nights out and cigarettes and clothes I barely wore) that the thought of giving all that up for the student life was not really appealing. I happily moved from one job to the next, mainly working in administration roles, behind a computer screen and dealing with customers over the phone. It was all pretty easy and wherever I worked, I always met really amazing people, and I enjoyed the social scenes that came with working in large corporations.

I also enjoyed the freedom that the money allowed for travel, and in 2002, like the big kids we were, Enrico and I decided to take a trip to Euro Disney in Paris. On the way home, we stocked up on about sixty bottles of wine at Calais, the French hub of duty-free goodies. I really don't know why we did it. I hated wine and Enrico didn't drink alcohol at all, but I suppose our inner *connoisseurs* believed we'd use it in all the restaurant-quality cooking we assumed we'd be doing now that were living together!

Occasionally, Enrico would open a bottle of red and add a splash of it to the spaghetti Bolognese sauce he was cooking and I would serve myself a glass of it to savour over dinner. It made a change from my usual weekend tipple of Malibu and Coke.

Then the odd glass turned into opening a bottle every three days, to eventually opening a bottle every night after I got home from work and polishing off the lot -- by myself. Within a short space of time, our wine supply was depleted so I would stop off at the shops on the way home from work and grab a bottle along with bars of chocolate, crisps and ciggies.

That had become my life. On autopilot.

It was only when one day I was taking the empties out to the glass bin that I realised just how much I was drinking. I had always been really sick on too much alcohol (especially wine) but it appeared that with all the drinking I was doing, I was building my tolerance to it. I had also only really ever been a weekend drinker, yet here I was, drinking every single night of the week.

What the hell was going on?

It was clear once I decided to get really, really real with myself.

I'd been distracting myself *from* myself and the unconscious unhappiness that I felt at not feeling totally fulfilled by life. I realised I had been numbing out for years. Looking for ways to avoid what I truly desired and following what truly lit me up. It all passed by in a hazy blur of life, as it often does.

Years of suppressing who I really was. Years of being the biggest people-pleaser ever known to man. Years and years of not speaking my truth and, instead, stuffing it down with food and alcohol and cigarettes.

But I could numb out no longer. It was time to make a change.

I believe that we are ALL born with this free-spirited nature; it's not just reserved for a few.

You only have to be in a room full of toddlers to see that children come into this world with the natural desire to be free to explore as they please. There is this innate tendency in children to just follow their highest joy and inspiration, even if it makes no sense to the adults around them. Their main pre-occupation is to play, explore, create, imagine, and create some more, build and laugh. It's what they LIVE for!

It's what we came into this world knowing was our purpose: to follow our bliss in pursuit of what lit us up most of all. To be who we truly are in each moment.

But as time goes on, this free-spirited nature tends to be socialised, traumatised or shamed out of them. Perhaps one day, when they were just being themselves, they were told to *stop being so weird and just act normal* (or something equally mean and soul destroying).

Or maybe there was an unspoken tone of disapproval in the air when they were acting in a way that was not in line with the ways everyone else in the family or community or culture acts.

So, instead of letting their spirit roam free, they start to conform out of fear of being rejected or cut off from love. This usually happens at some stage in childhood. It could be simply through being told to grow up or to act your age or stop being silly. Something that, whilst may sound harmless, is actually enough for a child to believe they need to be different. It could be that they observe how the grown-ups behave.

They notice that the gown-ups don't seem to want to play and explore or create and imagine, and create some more, or build and laugh.

It's likely that, at some stage in the grown-ups *own* life, their free spirited nature was squashed out of them, too, and as they grew up, they got caught up in the seriousness and busyness that they believed had to come with being an adult.

They learned to fit and follow the norms. They learned to follow the crowd instead of following the beat of their own drum, and, be it outwardly or inwardly, they *will* question what gives the free-spirit the right to be so frigging free-spirited.

What the heck gives them the right to walk to to do their own thing instead of being bogged down by the norm and the busyness and the seriousness of life? And because the crowd-follower has forgotten that, deep down, they are also free, they will look at the free spirits and say: *why can't just stop being so weird and just act normal for once?*

But that would be like a caterpillar being pissed at a butterfly for daring to be so bold and beautiful and free, when the caterpillar also has that capacity to fly and be free -- it just doesn't know yet. Throughout their life, the crowd-follower will be reminded of their own true nature and how to access it once more, though. They will hear a song that reminds them of how freely they used to dance, or they will read a book that will remind them of the days gone by when they would long to write stories and create amazing make-believe lands. This is an awakening.

Stop Letting People Treat You Like Crap

…because you deserve better.

There are some people you will encounter along your journey (or who perhaps may already be in your life) who, no matter what you do, find a way to put you down.

Not because they are triggered and working through their own stuff. Not because they are unconsciously projecting. Not because they are having a bad day or bad week.

Plain and simple, it's because they are arseholes.

It does not actually matter why they behave the way they do; it is NOT your responsibility to help them grow or heal or become a kinder person. Your only job is to stop putting yourself around those who put you down and belittle you and try to make you feel less than you are. You do not have to be anyone's energetic or emotional dumping ground.

It may feel like the hardest thing to do, but those who cannot love and respect who you are or how you feel do not deserve a space in your life and your heart. End of story.

Stop Waiting Until You Feel Fearless

…because it really is ok to be absolutely frigging terrified.

One of the biggest illusions is believing that, in order to be who you are and follow your dreams, you must first become totally and utterly, one trillion percent fearless. But it's an illusion because, as long as we are living, breathing beings with the capacity to feel the whole spectrum of human emotions, we will never, ever, ever become fearless. To me, it's the same as trying to be *sadless* or *angryless* or *frustrationless*.

I do realise that sounds ridiculous, but that is what it would come down to -- needing to be rid of a particular emotion to allow you to get on with your life rather than just embracing what you feel and why you feel it.

Maybe you believe that if you didn't feel fear you would just be living life exactly as you wished, merrily skipping along without a care in the word, doing all these seemingly scary things.

However, in reality, it's through acknowledging the fear, the sadness or the frustration that will free you -- not in aiming to get rid of the emotion altogether.

When I finally made the decision to stop talking about writing this book and actually wrote the damn book, I was still massively, massively, massively scared.

There was not a single day that went by when I wouldn't have that nagging voice in the back of my head and a sickening feeling in the pit of my tummy telling me all the reasons why it would be wiser to get over the fear *first*, why I had to wait and be perfectly ready before could move forward.

Every single day I had to face the part of myself that was absolutely horrified that I was making myself so vulnerable in sharing my true message with the world, the part where I was risking being judged, ridiculed and shamed for daring to speak what was in my heart. That part of me was horrified at the thought that sharing my truth like this would actually allow me to access the deeper, Infinite and Divine part of myself, rather than staying in my comfort zone of limitation and procrastination and distraction.

It was that part of me that would prefer I just did enough to feel like I was making progress without actually making any progress!

That's the thing. As you grow and evolve you'll realise that it's not *actually* the true you that is horrified, but it's a part of you that feels limited and feels like that your safety is going to somehow be compromised by you stepping out of your comfort zone (which is the home of The Limited Self.)

Your job is to keep moving forward anyway! To keep defying the part of you that would rather stay stuck forever.

The part of you that wants to remind you of your deep fears of not being strong enough, capable enough, brave enough, young enough, old enough, pretty enough or smart enough to be all you know you can be. Your job is to remember that these fears are not you and they are not true.

That's not to dismiss whatever has occurred in your life to create the fears in the first place or that you have no right to be fearful, but your mind has the ability to destroy your joy by either seeking to become totally fearless or becoming totally overwhelmed and fearful.

If you can just allow yourself to find the sweet spot between those two extremes, you will find yourself in a whole new energy where you will naturally reassure The Limited Self that everything is actually going to be ok. That going beyond where you have been before, beyond the fear, is 100000% ok, and there is no literal *life or death* situation occurring.

Over time you will find that, rather than becoming fearless, you will just fear *less*.

Things that used to stop you in your tracks will bother you no more and you will access a new level of courage that does not rely on you needing to dull your emotions, but rather one that allows you to feel them all and move the hell forward anyway, which is way more empowering!

SHINE A LIGHT

What have you been putting off pursuing because you felt that you needed to 'overcome your fear' first?

Stop Stop Stop Stop Stop Stop!

Stop denying your greatness. Stop denying your beauty.
Stop denying your wisdom. Stop denying your brilliance.
Stop denying your inherent worthiness. Stop denying your joy.
Stop denying your unique soul gifts. Stop denying your desires.
Stop denying your quirky nature (it makes you you).
Stop denying your inner wisdom.
Stop denying your natural tendency to thrive.
Stop denying your wellbeing.
Stop denying your ability to uplift by just being yourself.
Stop beating yourself up over your seeming imperfections.
Stop measuring yourself by what others accomplish.
Stop letting your past mistakes define who you are.
Stop holding onto things that don't make you feel good.
Stop trying to be all things to all people.
Stop putting yourself way down on the list.
Stop trying to diminish your light.

You are an infinite ball of cosmic stardust clothed in human
skin, and it's time to awaken to the magic flowing through you.

Today

Part Two

Honour

Honour Who You Truly Are

Imagine that, within you, you have this brilliant bright light that is waiting to be exuded at every opportunity. This light is your power, your strength, your creativity, your joy, your abundance, your beauty, your spirit, your MAGIC.

It represents everything about you that is Divine. That light is Your Divine Essence and it has always been inside of you, waiting to radiate and help you to live as the person that you came here to be.

But it's blocked by identities and fears and beliefs that you created because, somewhere along the line, you learned that it was not safe to be you in all your full radiant glory. That you have to hide or be someone different and that you need to protect yourself from further pain, and it's that pain that hides your light and hides who you really are.

Because those identities (or what I refer to as **parts**) are born out of trauma and pain and insecurity, they can be in total conflict with who you truly are and, as such, wreak havoc within you (which is why you may have learned to try to reject that part of you).

We could say that these parts are actually emotions and the ones that tend to stop us from moving forward are usually connected to a story that you have created following a trauma or the memory of a painful event in your life.

As you continue to move through this book, you will start to recognise the identities that you may have created within yourself and how they may be sabotaging your life.

Through the process of healing those wounds and reconnecting with our light (and, therefore, ourselves), we begin to see and release the identities that no longer serve us.

The identity that I found extremely hard to let go of was the *nice girl* identity. I've always felt that I needed to make sure others felt safe and happy. I was a nice girl, and being a nice girl meant that I was liked. Finally letting go of that identity was in equal measures of terror and liberation.

That sounds mega dramatic but it was like I had to let go of all the things I associated with being that *nice girl*. Things like, *nice girls* don't swear or get mad or tell people when they've been rude or say NO...and the list goes on and on.

I believed for so long that if I stood up for myself and spoke my truth (especially if it made others feel uncomfortable) I was essentially a really un-nice person. I felt that I got love and acceptance from being a bit of a doormat, so to stop letting others walk all over me felt like a recipe for total rejection and disapproval.

But when I started my healing journey, I had to let go of who I thought I needed to be.

Shine And Don't Give A Shite

I had been honouring what I thought others wanted me to be so, in essence, I had been honouring them first.

I had been ignoring my own inner knowing, neglecting my truth and downplaying aspects of myself.

I had been abandoning myself and rejecting myself time and time again in order to avoid the one thing I was most terrified of: being abandoned or rejected by others.

I was not able to fully honour who I truly was whilst I was being someone that I was not. The ME that I had been being for the majority of my life was (in every way possible) in conflict with the free-spirit I knew I truly was.

Somebody who could live their life without worrying too much about what people think and who could shine freely and fully without fear that somehow doing so was bad and wrong and was unfair to others.

I decided once and for all to choose being **me,** and I have been choosing to be more **me** every single day since. I can tell you there was so much liberation in breaking free from those old identities because I just knew that holding onto them was holding me back in so many ways.

What I know for sure is that, if you're suppressing who *you* truly are, then you're suppressing your light, your gifts, your awesomeness, and you are depriving the world of the magic sauce that only you can bring to the table.

So, what are some of the identities that are holding your back from being who *you* truly are?

Do you feel you need to live up to the image of *being perfect* or *Superwoman* or a *hard-worker* or a *domestic goddess* or a *nice girl* like me?

Maybe you've over identified with that part of yourself for so long that it feels weird to suddenly strip it away and become someone completely different.

After all, what would everyone else think and feel if you suddenly shed the layers of identities that you have been presenting and, instead, just allowed yourself to be who you are?

How would it affect those relationships that were built on you being the *limited* version of yourself?

Do you feel like you'd be judged, rejected, outcast?

Something that can hold us back from being true to ourselves is definitely the negative consequences we perceive will come from stripping away the identities that we have so far built ourselves and our lives upon. It really is enough to keep people living a lie for the whole of their lives.

But what if you actually started focusing on the positive consequences of you being who you really are?

How could you positively impact the world when you allow yourself to be you rather than hiding and being someone you are not?

What possibilities will become available to you when you decide that being who you are is utterly non-negotiable?

Shine And Don't Give A Shite

Oh for fuck's sake Kirsty, you're such an idiot. I snapped at myself.

The words flew out of my mouth so automatically, as they probably always do when I screw up.

In the moments before my little accident, I had been contemplating how easy it is to beat ourselves up when we make mistakes, and instantly I was served an immediate opportunity to see where I do that to myself!

It was so eye-opening. How could I really be loving to myself *and* tear myself to shreds over such a minor thing? It was literally spilt tea (albeit, spilt tea now seeping its way into my underwear drawer. Eeeew.)

As soon as I realised the power of my words, I took them back and apologised to myself, and wow, was it incredible. All of a sudden, I was free to just grab a cloth and clean up the mess.

No harm done. No big deal. No dwelling on it for the rest of the day or using it as a perfect reason to start listing in my head all the other reasons why I suck.

That's the immense power of honouring our imperfections. We no longer get to use them as a stick we yield every time we wanna beat ourselves up about something. We don't need to define ourselves by them.

I can be clumsy, messy, random, forgetful, disorganised; you name it. I am late, I speak without thinking, I have a tendency to apologise an inordinate number of times each day, and I am a major, major, lastminute.com person.

But do you know what? I have realised that none of that takes away from the fact that I'm also kind, funny, loyal, loving, encouraging, compassionate, fun and creative.

I would actually say that the things I used to consider my imperfections, the things I believed were flaws are EXACTLY what makes me uniquely me.

Even those parts of myself that I sometimes don't want to admit to. The parts of me that are not just messy and clumsy but are bitchy and judgmental and mean-spirited.

Those parts of ourselves that seem less like character flaws and more like shadowy, hidden and sometimes shameful traits that we bury and try to reject.

Remember, we are multi-faceted beings. We have the capacity to hate as much as we have capacity for love. We have the ability to destroy as much as we have the ability to create.

So much of the time we are encouraged to focus just on our light but it is in our darkness that we can truly access the depths of who we are.

It is only through truly acknowledging the parts of ourselves that we feel others would reject us for that we can truly be free to let go of anything that is stopping us from being who we truly are.

What would happen if you completely loved and accepted the aspects of you that you find totally and utterly imperfect and unacceptable?

That may feel counter-intuitive or that by acknowledging what has been kept in the shadows will somehow make you a bad person, but I believe that when we can truly love ourselves, we can begin to heal any aspect of ourselves that may be hurting.

You will never feel fully free until you embrace **every** aspect of yourself, every single part of you that you were led to believe made you unlovable or unworthy.

This, I now know, is where radical transformation happens. Not when we love ourselves *in spite of* those parts we feel make us deeply imperfect and flawed but *because* of them.

So much of the time we can stay in a cycle of self-hatred and punish ourselves for things that have happened in the past that we feel unable to forgive ourselves for.

We forget it is human to make mistakes. To fuck up. To do something so awful that we think there is no coming back from it. I don't know a single person who has never done something that they feel will define them forever, but it's how we deal with those mistakes that determines whether we grow or not.

If you beat yourself up, you don't grow.

If you deny it, you don't grow.

If you refuse to own it, you don't grow.

If you try to project it onto someone else, you don't grow.

It is 10000% ok to take full responsibility for your mistakes and go on to live your life.

Of course, that's not to say that we don't need to make amends or apologise or correct things. **It means that you get to embrace all aspects of your humanity and forgive yourself.**

If you feel a part of you trying to resist loving all of you, stop and just allow the feeling to come up. If you're not ready for that, allow yourself to be ok with not being ready for that. Or maybe ask yourself if there is something you need to forgive yourself for.

This process can be deeply painful, so don't force it. But if you are open to seeing it, you will be shown the ways you are hiding from yourself or punishing yourself because you are trying to reject a part of yourself that you find too much to bear.

This may sound heavy and deep but think of it this way: if you are rejecting any part of yourself, do you really think you will allow yourself to be truly you and live a life that you love?

The chances are that those parts of yourself that you see as imperfect are exactly what will set you free because you will no longer have to hide or shrink or dim because of them.

The main thing is to go through the work in this book with as little judgement for yourself and your imperfections as you possibly can because that is where true healing and letting go happens. It also allows you to see yourself from a more loving and compassionate vantage point, something that would not go amiss if you've been walking around thinking that there is something wrong with you for most of your life.

Allow yourself to accept all parts of yourself with total love and watch your life begin to transform.

"Within our shadows exists an opportunity for us to LOVE ourselves more."

Depika Mistry

Honour Your Inherent Worthiness

One of the reasons that someone may be fearful of shining brightly and being who they are is their belief in the complete lie that they are not good enough or capable enough or *whatever* enough for all they want to be, do, have or experience.

That, somehow, they have not yet earned it or are not deserving or allowed to be who they are or live the life they really want to live. I believe, in fact, I KNOW, we are all born with an inherent worthiness. We do not have to prove our right to thrive or be loved or be happy; we already *are* worthy.

Think about it for a second. When a baby is born into the world, at what stage of their life do they become worthy of being cuddled and loved and fed and kept safe? And what do they have to do to earn this?

The fact is, they are born *already* worthy of all of that, and when you were born, you were worthy of all of this, too. There was nothing you needed to do to prove that you were enough, you just were enough. NO QUESTIONS ASKED.

I believe that babies are born with a deep inner knowing that they are enough and that they worthy of all the attention and affection inevitably bestowed upon them.

Births are celebrated because, as humans, we acknowledge the magic that new life brings. We revere the specialness of a new person entering the world, and as such babies are showered in an abundance of gifts.

In fact, when my daughter was born, I was overwhelmed with the generosity of friends and family, and in some cases, people who I had never met who wanted to pass a blessing and gift on for Libby.

And there is a reason for this. We know inherently that the baby is worthy of all of that love. So, why would they ever stop being worthy?

I believe that it is when growing up that we begin to lose this sense of worthiness and the ramifications of that can be seen in small ways throughout our lives. Someone offers to help you out and you refuse the help. Or someone wants to treat you to something special but you feel like you can't receive it.

I have experienced this a lot in my life. I used to feel bad about receiving because I honestly felt like I didn't deserve it, but it was exactly that…_I_ felt like I didn't deserve it.

Why? Because I had this long-standing, deep core belief that told me I was not good enough. It is the degree to which _you_ feel good enough that will determine how much you allow yourself to receive all the blessings that life has to offer.

Ask yourself: *do I feel worthy?*

That is one of the most important questions to be addressed because, in order to shine and live the life you desire, you have to know that you are already worthy of that.

It will be apparent in the way you talk about yourself in your own head when you consider moving forward in the way you know you want to.

The thing is, when we get really quiet, we hear what we actually think about ourselves and, even though that can be horrifying, it can also be extremely enlightening.

For so much of my life I have felt this sense of unworthiness and I would try to prove my worthiness through how hard I was working or how nice and accommodating I was being to others or how much I was liked.

It was so eye-opening to realise that I was placing my value on things that were outside of me. Things that could not possibly dictate my worth.

One day in meditation, I realised just how much I was punishing myself by not allowing myself to receive and was instead caught in this cycle of needing to prove myself worthy *first*.

I saw what a complete trap this was -- and a never-ending trap, at that. I understood that, if you do not feel inherently, fully and undoubtedly worthy, you will constantly be trying to justify your life and prove your right to live it.

Shine And Don't Give A Shite

Not only is that massively exhausting, but I believe that this constant need to prove yourself can drive you into a place of burnout or breakdown. Neither is a pleasant place to be. As you begin to notice all the ways you may be holding yourself back from receiving, you will become more aware of why you feel so unworthy in the first place. You might be reminded of times in your life that you have made mistakes or done something you feel made you undeserving.

Maybe someone close to you told you that you didn't deserve something and you are still carrying this around as truth.

Maybe, as a kid, you saw your parents trying to prove their worthiness by not allowing themselves to receive and you took this to mean that it had to be that way for you, too.

Or maybe you will never discover why you feel unworthy, but none the less, you will realise that you can now choose how you want to feel going forward.

You get to choose between continuing to engage in the never-ending loop of denying your inherent worthiness or just accepting that you are as worthy today as the day you were born.

You have to honour your inherent worthiness. As you begin to replace those feelings of unworthiness with the image and sensation of your complete and utter worthiness, your life will become MAGICAL beyond measure.

SHINE A LIGHT

Do you feel worthy of all that you desire?

"You are worthy and deserving because you are an expression of divine love. You are worthy and deserving because your courageous heart beats."

Lee Harris

Honour Your Need to Belong

Let's be honest. No matter how much of a free-spirit you are or how much of a rebel you may be, the fact that you are reading this book shows me that you have been seeking the approval of others, trying to fit in or seeking validation for longer than you would have liked. I have discovered that one of the reasons that so many of us fall into this trap is our deep inherent need to *belong*.

In his paper *A Theory of Human Motivation** the late psychologist, Abraham Maslow, claimed that humans are motivated to satisfy a hierarchy of five basic needs.
These needs are usually depicted as a pyramid. The lowest levels of the pyramid are made up of the most basic needs (and must be satisfied first), while the most complex needs are at the top of the pyramid.

His theory is that, after our physiological and safety needs are met, we humans need to feel a sense of belonging and acceptance among social groups, whether these groups are friendships, family, cultural, religious or other.

*Maslow, A. H. (1943). *A Theory of Human Motivation*

He also claims that our need to belong is a more inherent need than our needs for esteem and self-actualisation.

This, I feel, deeply explains why it is so easy to fall into needing the approval, acceptance and love of others, even if it comes at the expense of our own sense of self. In essence, this need to belong is a *survival need* and it can also be explained through the theory of *tribe mentality*, something that I find extremely fascinating.

If you have ever watched the classic Disney movie *Beauty and the Beast*, you will have witnessed an example of that *tribe mentality* at play within the opening scenes of the movie. The townsfolk, all singing in unison, declare how strange and odd and peculiar Belle is for not being part of a crowd and for not fitting in like the rest of them. Instead, Belle is a character who walks to her own beat without apology (my kind of girl!) and just does her own thing.

The *tribe mentality* requires that all members of that tribe behave only in ways that are agreed upon by the tribe and conform accordingly (as in the movie where the townsfolk mainly see Belle as odd for not being like them).

Now, most of us are not living in tribes in the literal sense. And, unless it is cult-like in nature, even if we are part of any group (such as family, religion, friendships, work, etc.), individuality to varying degrees is most likely accepted. However, it is when someone has experienced (or witnessed) a negative response to individuality or breaking away from the norm that the feeling of fear of being rejected or abandoned by the groups we belong to may arise.

Shine And Don't Give A Shite

Honour Your Own Path

There is no shame in where you have been, where you are going or where you are right now. What matters most is allowing yourself to make peace with all aspects of your journey, no matter how shitty, painful or disappointing it may have been.

Maybe you feel that where you are right now is just a big pile of poo and you can't understand why you are not moving forward more quickly.

I totally understand how that feels. For the 18 months or so that I was planning and writing this book, I felt like I was just spending my days trying to wade through mud. My connection to myself seemed have been lost altogether, the client work that I had been doing up until that point had come to a stop, and it felt like I had no drive to put myself out there. I felt so frustrated that I seemed to have lost my drive and all I could think about what how much further along I *should* have been.

What I wasn't taking into consideration was the fact that I was going through the BIGGEST healing journey of my life. I was shedding emotional layers that I didn't even know were there.

Instead of just embracing where I was in that moment, I was in complete and utter resistance to everything. Wanting it to be different or make sense because it just felt too damn uncomfortable to not be where I thought I *should* be.

I soon learned that if I was in resistance to **any** part of my journey, I would continue to stay stuck because, as they say...

...what you resist persists.

Your journey is unique to you, and there is something magical that occurs when we can embrace that rather than resisting and fighting against it. As you make peace with that, the more expansive and enlightening your experience will be.

When you beat yourself up for not being further along than you are, you literally diminish the value of all the micro steps, courageous acts and bold actions that you took to get where you are right now -- as if your journey does not matter one bit, when, of course, it does.

The juice is in the journey. Enjoy and relish every step, honour how far you've come with grace and gratitude, and trust that your magical path will continue to be illuminated for you.

Know that wherever you are on your journey is exactly where you're supposed to be. How do you know? Because you're there. It may not look exactly the way you thought it would but just trust that you will be guided and, sooner or later, it will all make perfect sense.

Honour Your Divine Soul Gifts

So much of the time we are in denial about our own gifts because we have hidden them away for so long. They become buried in our memories, filed in the mental filing cabinet entitled: *Who I Once Was.*

The truth is, the things that make you, **you** cannot actually be hidden or forgotten. They are Your Divine Soul Gifts and the reason you were blessed with them in the first place is because they are the route through which you (and only you) can light up the world.

If you have some spiritual amnesia going on and really can't remember what Your Divine Soul Gifts are, think back to when you were younger and try to recall the things that you used to love doing more than anything in the whole wide world!

Your gifts may not even necessarily be tangible things either. For me, as a kid I loved being outside in my garden. I would talk to insects and collect leaves and climb trees. Sometimes I would take a bedsheet from my parents' room and drape it over the washing line, creating a makeshift tent, secured with a collection of rocks I had found that day.

I would sit in there and read for hours or find some other place where I could escape, be by myself and explore my rich inner world filled to the brim with ideas and infinite possibilities.

Although it may be tricky to see how this could really constitute as being gifts, it made me a very reflective, highly creative and deeply imaginative young girl.

And it's through my connection to myself that I can create and write and see past the realms of reality in ways that might not come as easily to others. Equally, it's through re-connecting with those things that once lit *you* up that you will light up the world in ways that neither I, nor anyone on the face of the Earth ever could.

Perhaps your gifts are something as obvious as being a fantastic writer or singer but please don't discount things like being a kind person or having a beautiful smile or being someone who can light up a room or lift the mood in any given situation.

Think about all the things that others have complimented you on before or consider what makes you feel so lit-up and excited inside that you would do it all day, every day given the chance.

Ask yourself: *What makes me uniquely special?*

Really spend some time with this question. Don't just brush it off because you feel uneasy at the thought of having to focus on the amazing things about yourself. Seriously, this task is so powerful. You are literally giving the parts of yourself that you have kept locked away permission to come back out to play, whilst rediscovering just how important owning your gifts and sharing them with the world truly is.

"*A musician must make music, an artist must paint, a poet must write, if he is to be ultimately at peace with himself.*"

Abraham Maslow

Honour Your Extra-Sensory Gifts

When many of us were raised, we were taught a system of beliefs. We were maybe told something along the lines of, *this is the way the world is* or *this is what we believe so this is the truth.*

Unless those beliefs are questioned, often they get passed from one generation to the next. One such belief is that the world is only what we can perceive with our five (agreed) senses. Those are the senses of sight, hearing, taste, touch and smell. Some claim that unless you can see it, hear, taste it, touch it or smell it, **it** is not real.

But oh, how those of us with extra-sensory gifts know otherwise (and when I say extra-sensory gifts, I'm referring to those that go way *beyond* the five senses we are mostly taught to be the <u>only</u> senses).

Now, some rational-minded individuals who have never accessed their extra-sensory gifts may argue that, unless you can prove it, it can't be real. And, to those individuals, I would say, imagine trying to prove that clouds or rainbows or stars exist to someone who has never been able to see, or to explain what LOVE is to someone who has never felt it.

Try proving that roses have a beautiful aroma to someone born without a sense of smell. That's how difficult it is for someone with extra-sensory gifts to prove what their senses are picking up on as well.

It's usually that skepticism from another that will cause someone to stop believing that their own extra-senses are actually real, which is usually when they suppress them.

Growing up with brothers, I tried to fit in with what they were doing. We'd build dens, climb trees and play on our bikes but I really loved being in my own little world. It was when I was alone, and especially in nature, that my extra-sensory gifts would come to life.

It started when my ears would tune out the noises of world around me and I would enter this totally different state. As if I were tuning into a new channel on the radio or, more aptly, a new frequency.

I now connect that feeling with being in a state of meditation but at the time I had no idea what was going on. I could bring this state on when I wanted to, and when I did, it felt like time would stand still.

It happened a lot at school.

I'd look around and notice everyone else just carrying on as normal, all the while thinking: *Can't you feel this? It's amazing!*

Each time I went into *my zone,* I came out feeling so connected to myself, like I just knew who I was beyond my worries and fears. It was like a reminder that I was safe and all was well.

I also noticed a deeper connection to nature. Trees felt more alive and being out in my garden was like a whole magical world.

More than that, I realised I could think about things happening and then they would! It was the funniest thing.

I'd have a thought that someone I knew was going to move house to a specific part of the city I lived in, and low and behold, they'd announce it a few days later. I'd pre-empt what someone was going to say just before they said it. It's like I could feel what they were feeling more than know what they were thinking.

One day, when I was about nine years old, two new boys joined my class. They were twins who'd recently moved over from Ireland.

At the end of every school day my brothers and I would walk the half-mile to another school where we would attend an after-school club called MASH. We'd play for a few hours before being picked up by mum or dad.

Whilst my brothers played footie, I'd find myself off on my own somewhere exploring. One afternoon, I had this thought right out of the blue. Well, not really a thought, more like an awareness: *The twins are going to join this club. Their mum is going to bring them here tomorrow.*

This would not be surprising if any children from my school were already attending the club but there were none. The majority of the children who went there were pupils of the school to which the club was attached.

None the less, even though they were brand new to my school and I had absolutely no reason to think they *would* be joining, I just *knew* they would be.

The next day, right on schedule, their mum strolled into the club with her boys in tow, asking how she could enroll them. I was excited to see them there but a bit freaked out. I mean, how on Earth did I know the day before that they were going to come today? No one had told me. I hadn't overheard anything. I just suddenly knew they would.

As time went on, I'd notice more and more occasions of things happening after I'd had the thought that they would. It was just something I could do. It was like *my magic*. I never thought to ask anyone else if they could do that. I just accepted it as one of those things. I now know it was my intuition, and it was coming through loud and clear!

When I began senior school, I had to start getting myself up and out of the house much earlier. I had this cool *Wallace and Gromit* alarm clock and, although it was funny to look at, the sound it would make to wake me up in the morning would really irritate me! As soon as it hit 7:00 a.m, Wallace's voice would repeat over and over and over again...

Come on Gromit, don't be a lazy-bones! (and if you've ever watched any of the films you can imagine the annoyance!)

It was enough to make me wanna hurl the thing out the bloody window, but as it was my only alarm clock, I had no option but to put up with it.

One evening, the thought of being woken by the Wallace's trill voice was too much to bear so I decided that I would use *my magic* to wake up by myself instead, on-time and before the alarm had a chance to go off!

Having always been a deep sleeper, it was something I'd never deliberately done before but I knew I only needed to trust myself and it would happen.

For the first few days I woke up with about 5 minutes to spare at 6:55a.m. It was like something inside would whisper in the sweetest of tones: *Come on Kirsty, don't be a lazy-bones!*

And up I'd spring out of bed feeling pretty damn victorious! I'd beaten the alarm clock! Wooohoo!

However, being someone who hates to lose precious sleep time, I wanted to get even closer to the 7:00 a.m alarm time. So before I went to bed, I started to tell myself that I would wake up just 1 minute before the alarm was due to go off, and true to my word, the next day I woke up at 6:59 a.m!

Sometimes there would be literally 10 secs to spare before I woke, which would give me just enough time to turn the alarm off before Wallace kicked in. It was like a game!

I began to trust myself completely and eventually stopped setting my alarm at all. Some may put this down to circadian rhythms but I knew I was connecting to a deeper part of me. It didn't matter what time I went to bed or what time I decided I wanted to wake up, as soon as I set an intention, a part of me would go to work to accomplish it.

Shine And Don't Give A Shite

It would be a whole two decades later until I discovered just how incredibly that power of intention would serve me in manifesting my dreams into reality.

But in the years between my teens and my early thirties, I really lost that connection to myself. I stopped trusting it so it stopped showing up. I became full of self-doubt and, although I would have the odd intuitive hunch, I would push it away. Deep down, I know that a part of me had to go through some time without it so that I could learn how to harness it in more powerful ways.

Which is exactly what happened when I met Alix.

Alix and I met through our lovely mutual friend, Helen, and as soon as I saw her I knew there was something very special about her. I couldn't put my finger on it at the time, but as I soon discovered that Alix was a deeply gifted intuitive, I instantly knew that that was what connected us.

She was also an incredible singer, and as a singer myself, it felt like I had been introduced to a long lost kindred spirit!

The timing of our introduction was especially synchronistic as I had set an intention just a few weeks before, that I wanted to have an intuitive guidance session. I knew I needed to connect with someone who would be able to help me understand some happenings that had occurred recently.

Since my daughter Liberty had been born a year earlier, I had this knowing that my nan, who had passed on in 2006, was around us. I could *sense* her and, as strange as this sounds, I could smell her perfume!

I also noticed that Libby was drawn to the vase that was sat on my windowsill that had once been my nan's and that I asked to keep after she had died.

There was something that becoming a new mum had activated in me and it ran way deeper than the magic I had experienced in my teens. I could now sense energy in a different way and I could tell that my extra-sensory gifts were evolving.

I excitedly booked a session with Alix, just knowing that she would be able to confirm what I was feeling. As soon as I sat down she started sharing with me the things she could see for me.

I had just returned to my teacher job after a years' maternity break and she sensed immediately that it was not aligned with me anymore.

She was able to tell me how much my stubborn, bossy attitude had been affecting Enrico of late (something that he himself had brought up to me just a few days earlier and I had vowed to change).

She also told me that I had this intuitive gift, too.

It was so amazing having someone who I didn't even know re-affirming to me what I was feeling, what was going on and what I was capable of.

What was truly amazing was what happened when Alix left the room to grab me a drink. Sat alone, I felt a shift in the energy in the room and when Alix came back smiling she asked me if I had any Celtic blood in me.

After initially not knowing what she meant, I suddenly knew exactly what she was going to say!

I confirmed that my dad's side of the family are Irish, and she said with a nod and a chuckle: *Ahh that explains it! A lady who I believe is your granny has been following me around my kitchen telling me I need to tell you she's here!*

My jaw almost hit the ground and I instantly felt a rush of energy like I had never felt surge through my body. It was like my intuition was on full force saying *YES! She is bloody right!*

I mean, Alix could not have possibly known that I was half-Irish just by looking at me. There are no clues. Taking more from my mum and her Caribbean heritage than my dad, I have dark skin, dark hair and dark eyes, I speak with a very English accent and, thanks to my hubby, I now have an Italian surname.

The fact that she described my nan's mannerisms, her physical appearance (and her forward nature!) down to a tee confirmed to me that she was not just making it up.

It was 10000000% confirmed when she also told me that my nan had been watching over Libby -- something that I had picked up on long before I met Alix, and something that, up until that point, I had not really told anyone about.

She also told me how much my nan loved me. Like really, really loved me. That was not a surprising message to hear; my nan and I were really close and I was there with her as she peacefully passed away in her own home six years before.

On the afternoon that she died, with her family around her, I received an intuitive nudge to start playing one of her favourite CDs -- a compilation of classic Irish folk songs. Even though she couldn't speak to me, I felt a strong knowing that she really wanted to hear that music in her final hours. It was, after all, the soundtrack of her life.

My nan always told me just how much she loved me, and a few days before she died, she told me how much it had meant to her that I had always been there for her. So to hear that she was around us was so comforting and confirmation of my own deep connection to the spiritual realm.

My session with Alix opened something magical within me. Not only did it remind me of the gifts I had inside me waiting to be shared, but she was the first person I had ever met who was owning her gifts with such boldness.

She was sharing her messages and owning her intuition in ways that were helping people reconnect with who they truly were, me being one of them.

It was in my second session with Alix a year later that she told me something that, again, no-one else knew. I had since left my job as a teacher and I had a deep desire to start using my own gifts of helping people tune into who they truly are and be who they were born to be. I saw myself running workshops, creating courses and writing books, but I felt like I had no right to do that when I was not even being totally true to myself.

Without missing a beat, as soon as I sat down Alix said, *I've been tuning into my Spidey-senses, Kirsty, and I can see that you wanna start running these women's workshops…but you're scared.*

It was another jaw-hitting-the-ground moment. I mean, how could she possibly know that?! It wasn't something I had put out there, but Alix could feel it. She just knew. I felt sooooo electric! And that surge of energy that I had felt move through my body in our first session zoomed through me again. It was my own intuition speaking up telling me that, again, she was spot on.

Fast-forward six months later and I was hosting my own workshops. I hosted fifteen that year; I also created four online courses helping people to connect with themselves, and I started taking on one-to-one clients with whom I would hold sessions on a regular basis.

Initially I would consider what I was doing as life-coaching because it felt like the thing that most easily explained it. In reality, I knew it wasn't that at all. I had started offering my clients intuitive guidance throughout our calls.

I would be mid-conversation with someone who would be sharing with me a fear or something that they wanted to do but had no idea how to move forward with, and all of a sudden, I would get that knowing. Something telling me what to say. Usually the thing I needed to say seemed so random and out there that, often I found myself holding back from sharing it, worried that I would overstep the mark or upset them.

But when I actually brought myself to say it, it would be met with total confirmation that what I had said was exactly what they were feeling or thinking or just what they needed to hear. The more open someone was in their own energy, the deeper that connection would be and the more intuitive insights would come flowing through me.

Just like Alix had done for me, I was now helping people to really know what deep inner beliefs and fears were keeping them from being who they truly were and sharing their own gifts with the world.

I share this because I have a strong feeling that if you felt drawn to me and drawn to this book, there is a very likely chance that you too possess extra-sensory gifts.

The vast majority of the people I have worked with and who have joined my workshops or even followed my work tend to be very, very intuitive in nature. They have this sense that there is waaaaaay more to life than what meets the eye (or any of the five senses for that matter!)

Some may have experienced things as a child that gave them this knowing. Some may have never tapped into their extra-sensory gifts but know that there is something waiting to come through them. Some are totally friggin' owning all of themselves and are boldly sharing their gifts with the world.

You may be reading all of this and doubting whether you have any of these so-called gifts at all but I believe, on some level, we all do. We just have varying degrees. For many, I believe it presents itself through just having an intuitive feeling about something, and the more connected to yourself you become, the stronger those feelings will become.

Just know that, as you start learning to trust your intuition, you are learning to trust yourself. And in a society where we are taught to look outside of ourselves for all the answers, being in touch with and living from your own inner guidance, implicitly, is, in my opinion, beyond courageous.

Shine And Don't Give A Shite

Honour Your Unique Calling

Your Unique Calling is the essence of your combined gifts and your unique personal qualities all rolled into one big bundle of magic stuff. But I do get that the idea of having a calling can seem quite overwhelming, especially if you have no idea what that means or what yours specifically *is*.

I had an epiphany a while ago when I realised that a calling is way less about what we are here to *do* and is actually everything to do with who we are here to *be*. It's the wellspring from which you will share your light but, ultimately, unless you own it, you will never fully be who you truly are.

You may have a sense of what Your Unique Calling is, but if you have this nagging feeling within you that you are not really living your purpose, it is likely that, on some level, you are afraid of fully owning it.

I believe that's because the bigger the calling feels to you, the stronger your resistance to stepping into it will be. So, the more your calling is going to help shift the vibration of the planet and help awaken others, the more terrifying it will feel to actually embrace it!

But it's not really something that you need to figure out. It will just be something you naturally embody the more *you* you allow yourself to be!

That's the great thing about it. You can just chill, and as long as you are doing what you can to be true to yourself, Your Unique Calling will be revealed to you.

My Unique Calling is to be an example of what it means to live in truth and light and heart and soul without apologising for it, and this book is a byproduct of me honouring that calling.

It is my deepest passion to help people step into the fullness of who they are, and I am especially passionate about understanding the ways in which we can nurture young children and teenagers so that they KNOW from as early on as possible that they are already worthy and enough, and that it is ok for them to be who they are.

Although I am a qualified teacher, I knew that the way in which I can serve best is not in the classroom teaching all subjects but in focusing on the topics that help me honour my calling and help the children I work with.

My job as a teacher (which I absolutely loved!) taught me that the most important thing we can teach are the things that help children feel good about themselves first.

That encourage them to feel connected and safe to be themselves, and that help them know what makes them special and unique.

Moments earlier, I had just been thinking about how much I was enjoying this writing process, so this was a big surprise to have this sudden moment of anxiety.

My usual mode of defense for such a thought would be to rationalise, to reason, to argue, to defend.

But instead, I allowed the thought to just be there, and the more I let it be unchallenged, unaltered, unquestioned, the less I felt the need to resist it. The more I let it simply breathe, the more at peace I was becoming with it and with myself.

It didn't take me long to detect bullshit as I realised this was actually *my* belief coming up out of nowhere.

It wasn't: *some people think that what I'm doing is a waste of time*.

It was: *I think what I'm doing is a waste of time*.

I had a fear that my book was going to be a waste of time.

That fear had been nestled snuggly away somewhere waiting to reveal itself.

Such is what happens when a fear is ready to be healed -- it will show itself at a time you are ready to see it and release it.

Before that time, there was no friggin' way that it would be a belief I would have been able to see, let alone own. But I was ready to face it full on.

I just let all the feelings and thoughts come up.

No one will read it...

It will be a flop...

People will think I'm a phony...

What if everyone disowns me for swearing so much?

And on and on it went. But instead of trying to rid myself of that fear by trying to push it away and brush it under the carpet, I just sat with it and allowed myself to fully sink into the fullness of the fear.

I sat and I allowed the feeling to be there, to just be present, and every time I felt a sense of insecurity, I would just let it be there. With each and every fear that I owned, I felt more and more free.

It was magical, and before long, the feelings were able to move through me and I could see them for what they were: just an indication of something inside me that wanted to be seen and heard. Like a child afraid of the dark who's fears do not subside by trying to push them away or being told to just grow up and get over it, but through realising that it's ok to be scared -- even if, in reality or to anyone else, it seems unreasonable.

By actually giving all of those fears room to breathe, they were suddenly free to leave and were replaced by a feeling of confidence that this book could actually be really good if I allowed myself to be ok with the fact that it might not be. But that feeling of confidence could only come once I had truly acknowledged **how I truly felt**.

Every day, as emotions rise up from inside you, you get the chance to practice being with whatever you are feeling in the moment, rather than analysing or rejecting those you feel are bad or wrong or cause you to feel discomfort.

It could be an aggressive conversation going on behind you that makes you feel nervous, or the memory of a past event that triggers a feeling of anger in the present.

It could be the feeling of unresolved grief that you have within you from when you lost someone close to you, or the sense of frustration that you feel around a scenario that is not going the way you'd prefer it to go right now.

Whatever it is, you have every right to feel it. There is no reason to believe that any feeling that may be deemed negative needs to be suppressed or pushed away. The key is letting go and surrendering into the emotion that is trying to move through you.

After all, the Latin derivative for the word emotion, (*emotere*) literally translates to *energy in motion*, meaning that emotions are supposed to flow through us so that they can be felt.

You may be wondering how this could possibly be related to allowing yourself to shine. We can be led to believe that shining is all about the sweet and light and positive-vibes-only kind of image, but seriously, nothing could be further from the truth.

Shining isn't just about beaming your brightest smile to the world, dressing up in tutu and tiara, riding unicorns or sliding down rainbows (although, how awesome would that be?!) It's about being you. Fully, wholly, completely you.

It's about realising that our emotions play a big part in that experience, and the only way to reveal who we truly are begins with letting ourselves feel how we truly frigging feel.

It could be that you are scared of looking within you out of fear of discovering an emotion that you have been burying out of a misguided belief that it was somehow an unacceptable emotion to express.

Real and in-the-moment emotions are what allow us to flow and grow and express ourselves. It's the trapped emotions, the ones we feel are somehow bad or wrong, that, if left buried, will make it hard for you to be fully you.

Have you ever experienced that? Have you ever had this niggling feeling brewing under the surface? Feelings of rage or sadness or guilt or shame or envy that, whenever it gets too close to the surface, you push down somehow.

But those deep, dark, secret feelings that you believe should not be seen or heard are actually trying to move through you. They are wanting to be seen and heard and released so that you can actually get the hell on with living your life. Because we both know that the thing you are doing to distract yourself from how you truly feel is having an even more devastating effect on your life than if you were to just let yourself *feeeeeel*.

Like I shared earlier, I avoided how I felt for long enough that I developed a drinking habit that, if left unchecked, would have spiraled way out of control by now. The long and short of it was, I was pushing myself into an early grave by not being fully honest with myself about how I truly felt.

Since the evening of My Divine Wake-Up Call, I have spent pretty much every single day sitting with myself and asking myself how I feel; what is going on inside that wants to be heard and seen and expressed and released? Every day I honour myself in that way so every day I grow and evolve.

I feel more at peace with myself and more connected to myself than ever before. I try to express what I feel rather than bottle it all up or avoid it because I know the pain that I put myself through by denying my true emotions.

Allowing yourself to shine means that you allow yourself to be exactly who you are in as many moments as possible, and a really important part of that is allowing yourself to feel every inch of how you feel, without apology.

It's about reclaiming your right to be a human being who came into this life experience with the capacity for a whole load of emotions that need to be expressed and felt.

It's about letting go of any bullshit stories that told you that feeling the way you feel is wrong, or that there are certain emotions that need to be suppressed or contained.

It's about authenticity over acceptability.

It's about vulnerability over vanity.

As you allow yourself to be someone who is ok with feeling how they feel, those emotions that feel stuck or perhaps are ready to move on will be released. The other amazing thing about being with yourself and letting yourself become acquainted with your emotions is that you will become really aware of any tendency to dismiss how you feel.

We can do this in an instant without even realising it.

Whenever you say, *I shouldn't be feeling this way,* about any emotion you feel is silly or pathetic or childish, you are diminishing your very valid emotions.

Remember, every emotion is valid.

Every emotion needs to feel embraced.

Every emotion wants to flow.

There are no *good* or *bad* emotions. It's all just ENERGY wishing to be expressed and moved through you.

Your job is to keep allowing that energy to flow so you don't become stuck and, over time, you will find ways to release the energy that are healthy and effective for you.

Just keep allowing yourself to feel how you feel, and whenever you catch yourself saying, *I shouldn't be feeling this way,* or *I should be over this by now*...STOP...take a deep breath and say...

...it really is ok for me to feel the way that I feel.

...because truly it is.

"The walls we build around us to keep sadness out also keeps out the joy."

Jim Rohn

Honour Your Healing Journey

The release of emotions that have been unexpressed within you is the journey of healing. It's about allowing yourself to just be open to feeling whatever comes up in the moment as opposed to carrying around a suitcase of emotions that weigh you down and make it difficult for you to live freely.

That's not to say that the objective is to try and offload all our emotions at once or that there is even a designated time-frame by which someone should feel emotions. It's a personal journey. What I have learned along this spiritual path is that expressed emotions are healthier than unexpressed emotions.

When you go through any healing journey you are basically releasing the stuff that's been hiding who you truly are and the layers of protection that you have used to keep you safe.

It is also about shedding all the layers that are currently hiding your light, your brilliance, your magic. These can be layers of limiting beliefs, fears, doubts, habits or relationships that don't support you. I do understand that even just the mere thought of venturing into these layers can be really uncomfortable, especially if there is trauma attached.

That is why I would really invite you to explore supported routes for healing, so that you do not have to go through it alone. You may decide that you want to work with a counsellor or therapist or wellbeing practitioner to help you work through what may seem like a daunting journey.

Throughout my own healing journey, I have worked with many healers. From Reiki masters, to reflexologists, to Emotional Freedom Technique practitioners to Beyond Quantum Healing to working with gifted initiatives (please refer to the Magical Resources section at the back of this book for details of amazing distance healers I have worked with and would massively recommend).

My path of healing was very spiritual (and, as you can see, quite alternative) because that is what felt right for me. Your path will be whatever feels right for you.

The main catalyst for my deeper healing was in following my own intuition and sitting and being with myself every day. I spend hours every day journaling and meditating and doing the things that help me connect with myself so that I can actually start to hear what it is that I need to hear.

This, I believe, is the most incredible thing we can do for ourselves. The power of self-healing (whilst not taking away from other modes of healing) cannot be underestimated.

Just allow yourself to fully honour your healing journey because, as you do, you will give yourself space and time to actually heal as opposed to feeling any need to sabotage it. Allow yourself to be supported as you move through it. You never need to do this alone.

Part Three

Illuminate

"And the day came when the risk to remain tight in a bud was more painful than the risk it took to blossom."

Anaïs Nin

Illuminate Even More

You may have found that revealing your deepest fear in the last chapter was pretty unilluminating!

Perhaps nothing came up or you feel like you just can't let yourself go there just yet.

That's absolutely not a problem.

Often our fears need coaxing out from the security blankets they have been hiding underneath, and you could do this by reflecting on a few more questions.

Well, you're in luck, coz I've come up with LOADS more!

I've phrased these from a second person point of view, so I am asking you rather than you asking yourself.

Sometimes this change of perspective can shift things up a bit, but if you prefer, you could just reword them.

Again, grab your journal, or mediate or dive straight in (you know the drill!)

Illuminate Your Next Steps

Wow! If you managed to get through even one of these questions, I applaud you. Doing this inner work is what will move mountains for you in your life. It takes a lot of courage to look at aspects of yourself that have, up until now, hidden, and the fact that you have begun the process is really awesome.

However, don't be alarmed if you start to doubt what came or find yourself sabotaging yourself over the coming days. Just be easy on yourself and remember why you are doing this.

Your next steps lie in chapters that follow this one where you will learn how to really **Nurture** and **Expand** your way into manifesting what you desire most whilst simultaneously releasing any fears that have held you back up until now.

It will also support you in stepping into the fullness of yourself so that you can allow what you desire to flow to you.

Keep in mind, it is a process to be respected, and as I've said a bazillion times, there really is no rush. Go at your own pace, but keep going, and know that your future self will be so thankful that you did this work!

Illuminate Your Powers of Manifestation

If you are someone who really needs to do something practical to anchor this all in, I would really suggest creating a vision board! If you have not created one before, it is really fun and it really works.

It basically consists of a digital or physical collage of images that represent your desires. These can be as obvious or abstract as you want (why so a Google search and see what comes up).

My first vision board contained a photo of an event that I really wanted to attend called A-Fest. It is an immersive 5-day experience that combines transformation with epic fun and is hosted by the company Mindvalley (Google them too!)

Back in 2015, when I created the vision board, I had no idea how getting to A-Fest would be an option for me. The ticket prices were out of my reach at the time, and as it would involve me travelling to Costa Rica for a week, it would mean leaving, my then, 3-year old Libby behind.

But even though there were obstacles, I remember frequently looking at that image on my board and holding the intention that I **would** go, and that the **how** would be taken care of.

Then one day, out of the absolute blue, I was generously gifted two fully paid for tickets to the event by a lovely lady called Bianca that I had only known for a few weeks!

IT BLEW MY MIND.

Especially as just a few days before, I'd had a conversation with my good friend Julie about my desire to go, but Bianca had no idea it was even on my radar, let alone my vision board!

Bianca explained that she had the deep pull to give the tickets to me after being unable to attend the event herself. I mean, you literally can't make this stuff up!

Not only did the tickets just fall into my lap, I also manifested thousands of unexpected pounds to pay for everything else I needed for the trip, and my mum was totally happy to take care of Libby whilst I was away.

This did not just happen to me coincidentally. I set a powerful intention for it to happen, created a vision for it happening and then let go of the outcome. I was not desperately attached to going to A-Fest but I was excited at the thought of it.

Even now when things like that happen it still knocks my socks off but it really is the incredible power that we all have inside us!

When you get super-duper clear about what you want, and you get into the energy of having it show up for you, that is when The Universe can co-create with you. But if you feel heavy and doubtful and fearful of allowing what you desire, you basically push it further away from you (energetically speaking).

Also, if you feel like your desire will complete parts of your life that you deeply feel are currently lacking, you are manifesting from a place of lack, which equals manifesting more lack.

Manifesting from a place of abundance feels free, light, fun, exciting, as if your desire is a no-brainier because, when you think about it, it feels the same way you already feel about your life. You are not looking for your desire to complete your life, instead you just feel lit-up at the thought of allowing it.

Match your vibration now to how you want to feel until you no longer need your desire to show up but you are still excited at the prospect of it. Only then can it show up.
There is an undeniable truth that has, so far, been the absolute MAGICAL key to manifesting awesomeness into my life (such as that incredibly life changing trip to Costa Rica)...

...you just have to know that what you desire is already yours.

Know that you are worthy of it. Stop the need to prove you've earned it or justify why you want it.

Have a deep knowing that it is already yours.

You may not know how it will show up but believe me when I say that letting go of how will be the best decision you make when it comes to allowing what you desire to enter your life.

Your only job is to hold your vision, hold the feeling of having it and hold the faith! And as much as possible, bask in the feelings of ease, gratitude, joy, flow, love and abundance **right now**, then watch as your life becomes magical beyond belief.

These are the messages that you need to start paying really close attention to as they are trying to guide you.

I know from my own experience that it can be really hard to decipher them and, often times, we can write all of that off to sheer coincidence.

When that happens, actually ask for guidance. Ask for clarity. Sit and meditate and pray and journal and be clear about what you want to know. Then listen for the answer. It may come through as a new awareness that just seems to pop out of nowhere. It might be delivered as a message from a friend. Or it could be something so obvious that you literally can't miss it!

Whatever it is, just trust it! And trusting it means actually taking the action that it is calling you towards.

My life became exponentially better moment by moment only when I started to follow my inner guidance and take the inspired action that I was being called to take. Yours will, too, if you take the steps you're being called towards.

It could just be one step. Like to call that friend you haven't spoken to in a while. Or go for a walk. Or change the channel on your TV. It might not make sense in that moment but it will at some point, I assure you. And the steps will lead you where you wanna go.

Learn to trust your own inner guidance system and life will become more and more magical as each day passes. But you don't have to take my word for it because, deep down, you already know the truth of this. You've just gotta start believing in that knowing for long enough to see it for yourself.

Part Four

Nurture

Nurture Yourself

We are living in a time where the importance of self-care is at an all-time high. There are so many advocates encouraging us to pour into ourselves and fill our own cups (so to speak), and I could not agree more.

Anyone who has found themselves at the brink of burn-out will know how vital taking care of oneself is. It is not just some luxury that we should apologise for indulging in; it is a necessity of life.

Nurturing yourself might look like having an early night when you are just beyond exhausted or nourishing your body with healthy, delicious, nutritious food.

It can also be treating yourself to a spa pamper day where you are massaged from temple to toes, or it could be just curling up on your favourite armchair with a blanket and listening to the rainfall.

Of course, bubble baths, country walks and a 10-minute tea break all help, but the type of self-nurturing I'm talking about goes way beyond that.

It's about taking the vast majority of the energy you have been pumping out to everyone and everything and redirecting it back to you.

And that might look radical in your life. It might look like reducing your hours at work in order to regain your balance. It might look like saying no to any social commitments for the next few months so that you can spend that time taking care of you and doing those things that totally align you back with who you are.

It might look like not being available to speak to every person who needs or wants something from you right now and being totally honest about needing time for yourself.

It's about allowing wellbeing in all its form to start flowing back to you without restriction, justification or apology.

Wellbeing is that feeling of being totally held and cared for and taken care of. It's that feeling of being supported by The Divine Flow, when life just seems to be tending to your needs, and you feel lit-up and expansive.

But we can resist this flow in so many ways. Yes, we can absolutely resist it through eating crap and poisoning our bodies with substances that cause us to feel run-down and disconnected.

We can resist wellbeing through staying up late at night and time again and refusing to rest when our bodies are beyond exhausted (guilty as charged).

We can resist wellbeing by busying ourselves all day long and multi-tasking our way through life.

All of these modes of resistance are simply symptoms of the main reason we don't allow ourselves to be as happy, vibrant, abundant and lit-up as we possibly can; the underlying reason I believe is a general feeling of unworthiness.

Feeling like you have not earned the right to have ALL of you needs taken care of. So you sabotage your wellbeing and you focus on all the reasons you don't deserve to experience the full magnitude of being in The Divine Flow.

When was the last time that you took a bath or put your feet up and then felt a pang of guilt because you were not doing something *more productive*?

How about the time you were feeling totally amazing in your body and then decided to eat, drink, smoke or ingest something that you just knew would make you feel like utter dung again?

Or what about all the ways you refuse to allow yourself to be supported by others, even when you could really do with the help?

Maybe you've got a million and one things to do, and someone reaches out to offer a hand, but instead, you say no and struggle to juggle it all yourself, as if it's some kind of endurance test.

No matter what your unique blend of sabotage is, the bottom line is it comes from a place of not feeling like you can just thrive in all ways. **But your mental, emotional, physical and spiritual wellbeing is extremely important.**

I went through an intense period of healing as I was writing this book.

I uncovered wounds and scars (many from past lives) that I didn't even know existed and, as I encourage you to do, I sat with them all and just allowed them to be present.

As a lot of my deep inner healing comes through sleep (which is why I now know I had been resisting sleep for such a long time), I would find myself needing to just stop typing and take a long nap. Usually this would be in the middle of the day while Enrico was at work and Libby was at school.

Even though my whole being was calling out for rest, for healing, I would resist out of a feeling of guilt.

I mean, why should I get to sleep right now when I should be working? How lazy am I?

Fortunately, the majority of the time, I would see that it was just my Limited Self's attempt to stay stuck and contracted, because it knew that sleep would lead me to a new place of expansion beyond where I had been.

So I would resist it only to find myself unable to keep myself awake come evening. But by hook or by crook, the part of me that wanted to heal would fortunately win, and I would awaken feeling so much lighter, freer, happier and more connected to myself.

That is the power of allowing yourself to nurture yourself. You will be showing yourself that you are frigging worthy of being taken care of, of sleeping or eating well or thriving. You will drop this strange societal notion that says that *sleep is for the weak* and puts struggling and running yourself into the ground up on a pedestal.

I mean, how messed up is that?

That somehow, the more we push and strive and force ourselves into depletion, the worthier we are. There is a skewed belief that is programmed into so many of us that says: *if I focus on myself, it makes me selfish* but nothing could be further from the truth.

How could it possibly be wrong or self-indulgent to look after yourself?

Nurturing yourself is not a selfish thing to do. It's the fair thing to do.

The more you nurture yourself, the more you will find yourself focusing less on *doing* and more on just *being*, and living life at your own pace.

Without feeling in any way guilty about it.

In fact, one of the most important and conscious decisions I made a few years back was to stop living my life at a pace that is deemed normal in society.

The rat-race pace.
The burn-out pace.
The super-woman pace.
The strive and achieve pace.
The get-shit-done pace.
The keeping up pace.
The multitasker pace.
The DOING pace.

Living my life at that pace meant that I had no capacity to fully nurture myself. So I now live life at MY pace.

The breathe-in-life pace.
The slow and steady pace.
The listen to my heart pace.
The life is not a race pace.
The present moment pace.
The chill and do-nothing pace.
The create when inspired pace.
The let's have fun and play pace.
The stop and smell the roses pace.

The BEING pace.

Sometimes I trick myself into thinking that I need to go back to the old way. The way that demands I put my wellbeing on the back burner in favour of a never-ending *to-do* list.

Then I remember how much that pace made my soul ache and my heart hurt from the stress and worry that somehow, even amid the chaos, I was still not DOING enough.

That's because we are taught that simply BEING is pointless, airy-fairy stuff of lazy bones and will never direct to what we need to accomplish in life. But I realised that it is when we have courage to STOP and take care of our wellbeing first and foremost that life becomes more balanced and way more fun!

SHINE A LIGHT

What could you do today to nurture yourself?

"It takes courage to say yes to rest and play in a culture where exhaustion is seen as a status symbol."

Brené Brown

Nurture Your Boundaries

For so much of my life I focused on being so accommodating and agreeable and nice that my boundaries were pretty much non-existent. I found it hard to say *no,* and in my quest to say *yes* to everything and everyone, I ended up depleted, burned-out and totally disconnected from myself.

It took me a looooooooong time to realise that if I really wanted to be true to myself and live life on my terms, I would have to set some strong-as-hell boundaries and honour them without apology. I had to be really clear about what was acceptable in my life and what was no longer acceptable.

I had to have some honest conversations with people who I had allowed to treat me in ways that did not make me feel good whilst taking full responsibility for the fact that, up until then, I had been more interested in protecting their feelings than my own. It was only when I considered that I was important, too, that things in my life started to massively shift.

If you know that you are not fully respecting or nurturing your boundaries, it may be time to have that honest conversation with yourself about where things are out of balance for you.

It could be that you have a particular person in your life that you feel unable to say *no* to when they ask for something from you.

Ask yourself: *what would be different if I actually spoke my truth to this person and told them not only how I feel, but also what I was no longer available for?*

Sometimes, for people-pleasers, the sheer idea of no longer saying yes to those we feel need us can feel so selfish. As if it is your duty to be more accommodating and available for others than you could possibly be for yourself.

That somehow your needs are less worthy or that it's your responsibility to be available no matter what it costs *you*. But when you constantly put other's needs above your own, it does cost you, and you are not considering the deeper impact of how saying *yes* when you mean *no* affects you emotionally.

You *are* worthy and you are important, and it is only when *you* honour that, that others will know to honour that, too. This is what nurturing your boundaries looks like. Knowing that it's ok to say no to things that deplete you, and knowing that it's ok to do things that fill your cup.

It really, really is ok to make yourself a priority because, let's be honest, if you are overworking, overcommitting, and generally *over-people-pleasing,* you will soon burnout and have nothing to give anyone anyway. So, don't be afraid to set boundaries. They are 1000000% necessary if you wanna step back into your power, shine your light and be true to yourself!

"As a self-celebrating, self-respecting individual, you WILL annoy some people. You will annoy A LOT of people. You will be misunderstood, perhaps thought of as arrogant. You may be uninvited. When you LOVE yourself enough to say, '*This is acceptable in my life and this is not*,' you will become unacceptable to other people, especially those who tend to push against your boundaries."

Danielle LaPorte

Nurture the Relationships that Nurture You

When you start connecting with yourself and releasing any stories that have kept you small, you will begin to notice those who you feel you still need to shrink around and those you can be your full, expansive, brilliant self around.

The latter people are your people. They are the ones who will forever be encouraging you to shine at your full capacity because, when you do, you remind them that they have the capacity to shine brightly, too. They are the ones that will be rooting for you to succeed in everything you do because you are there on the side-lines cheering them on as they embark upon their own journey.

The relationships in which you will thrive are the ones where you can be 100% yourself and the ones that you may naturally nurture over time. Either way, you deserve to feel fully supported and respected in EVERY SINGLE ONE of your relationships.

Don't settle for less than love because what you allow will set your worthiness barometer and determine what you attract back to you, guaranteed. So set that bar way high!

Nurture the Divine Spark Within You

From a young age, I remember being really interested and curious in things that connected me to My Divine Essence. As a teenager, I would be drawn to the crystal shop in the city centre that I grew up in.

If I worked the early shift in my Saturday job making sandwiches and preparing jacket potatoes for hungry shoppers, I would finish in time to pay the crystal shop a visit, eager to see what my day's earning could purchase.

As soon as I entered, I would be mesmerised by the beautiful, enchanting aroma of burning incense and dusty, mysterious books ready to be explored. Books on spirituality, meditation, healing and other intriguing topics. I would pore over the numerous different, weird and wonderful artefacts on display, feeling this warm and fuzzy feeling, like a spark, welling up inside of me telling me that this was home.

Over my trips to the shop, I bought a book on meditation, which came with a CD, a handful of beautiful crystals and hundreds of sticks of incense. It was a kind of sanctuary away from the busyness of the market streets.

I found myself fascinated by anything alternative, anything that sought to explain the mysteries of The Universe. I had always had a deep connection with what many refer to as God, but for me, despite my Christian upbringing, I did not relate at all to the notion that God was some man up on a cloud.

I knew there was something deeper than that. I could feel it, and I knew that it was only to be discovered the more I nurtured that spark within me, The Divine Spark that is always connected to the Source of all that there is.

I knew that it was way more important for me to connect with that feeling as much as I could and let myself be guided by it rather than be told what to believe and what God was or was not by other people.

I had a sense that we are all connected to this spark and that we awaken to it by paying attention to when we feel those awe-inspired moments. For some, that could be in church, or temples, or sacred spaces of deep reverence. For others, it could be in listening to music, meditating, sitting in nature, painting, praying, chanting, singing, exploring crystal shops... the list goes on and on.

The point is, (and this is my personal opinion) there is no right or wrong way to nurture and connect with that spark within you.

For those of us who have felt a deep spiritual connection in ways that go against traditional religious beliefs, it can be confusing to go against what we were taught. It can also make someone doubt themselves and their feelings.

My biggest shift came when I decided to let go of any need to follow the beliefs of anyone else and instead trust that the feelings of love and peace and joy were enough of an indicator that what I was feeling was real and valid, and that it was important for me to nurture it.

It *is* so important to nurture that Divine Spark within you, in ways that matter to you. Even if it goes against the grain of what you were told you should do or what you were told you should believe. The more you nurture that spark, the more it will grow, and you will find yourself radiating the energy out into the world.

Trust that what lights you up and helps you feel connected to Your Divine Essence may be totally unique to you, and that is totally fine. I honestly don't believe there are any rules. I believe we are all here to experience that incredible Divine source energy in our own unique ways. Not just in one way that we are all *meant* to follow.

What I *have* found is that, anything that ignites that spark will generate feelings of love and joy and excitement within you in such a way that you can't help but be drawn to it. It may not even be in any way a religious or spiritual connection. That spark can be ignited in some in what others may see as the mundane or the simple.

For me, it's not only when I find myself in shops filled to the brim with all things mystical that I feel that spark. I feel it when I take a stroll on a beach or immerse myself in nature or read a good book or go to an intuitive dance session (hell yes to 5Rhythms!)

I feel it when I'm singing Frank Sinatra at the top of my lungs, or camping out under the stars in the British countryside, or when I'm splashing in puddles and making forts in the living room with Libby, or bantering with Enrico, or jamming with a funky band, or sipping cocktails with my friends, or watching re-runs of my favourite films and comedies, or travelling, or big family functions, or teaching children to sing, or going to the theatre, or meditating, or putting my bare feet on the moist morning grass, or eating incredible Thai food...the list goes on and on and on.

The point is, it really does not matter what anyone else thinks about what lights that spark for you because no one else can feel that connection you feel in the exact way you do.

My deepest belief is that we are all Divine in nature.

It's who we are at our very core and essence and how we choose to connect with our Divinity that is unique and personal to each individual. I don't believe that such an amazing connection could possibly be reserved for just a few.

What matters is that you remain true to you, no matter what because, in doing so, you will be internally guided to your ultimate truth. Just keep following that spark.

SHINE A LIGHT

What lights the Divine Spark within you?

"Let yourself be silently drawn by the strange pull of what you really love. It will not lead you astray."

Rumi

Shine And Don't Give A Shite

Nurture Your Vision

One of my favourite movies ever is *The Pursuit of Happiness,* starring the awesome Will Smith. The film depicts the real life story of a man called Chris Gardner who, in the 1980s (along with his young son Christopher), found himself homeless.

It's such an inspirational story because, despite not having anywhere to live and barely enough money to buy food, Chris stays optimistic that things will get better. His positive, proactive attitude lands him an opportunity to be a stockbroker for one of the biggest firms in San Francisco but first, he has to go through a grueling and unpaid 6-month internship.

I love the movie because Chris kept believing in his vision and what was possible for him, even if his current situation appeared to indicate that he and his son were doomed.

I won't give the ending of the movie away but let's just say that the real-life Chris Gardner is now a multi-multi-millionaire and one of the most sought-after motivational speakers in the world. His story is filled with so many highs and lows, and it really is a movie that keeps your emotions running.

For me, the most powerful scene is when Chris and his five-year-old son, Christopher (played in the movie by Will's real son, Jaden Smith), are out on the court playing basketball.

Little Christopher (who clearly has some young Fresh Prince b-ball skills) enthusiastically tells his dad that he's *going pro,* to which his dad dismissively responds that, due to his own average basketball skills, his son should not expect to excel in the sport either. That he shouldn't waste his time even practising.

Clearly disheartened, Christopher starts to put his ball away, no longer wanting to play. After a moment's pause, and upon realising that he had potentially crushed his son's passion, Chris looks Christopher in the eye and tells him to <u>never</u> let anyone convince him that he's not capable of doing something, and that, if he has a dream, he must protect it.

Those words of wisdom spoken from father to son have resonated with me all these years. I know first-hand how easy it can be to doubt your own vision and allow yourself to water it down or be influenced by someone else's view of what is possible for you.

Just remember, nobody else can see what you see, and it is not their job to either! It's only your job to totally trust in and nurture your own vision for your life, and only then will it come to fruition.

<u>SHINE A LIGHT</u>

Do you believe in your vision or are you waiting for others to believe in it before you fully believe in it yourself?

"Whatever you can do or dream, you can, begin it. Boldness has genius, power and magic in it."

Johann Wolfgang von Goethe

Nurture Your Creativity

Time and time again I hear so many people say that they are *not creative in the slightest*. However, I know that it is our ability to create that allows us to manifest our desires into our lives. We are, after all, co-creating our realities with The Universe.

That's why I believe that being creative is not a standard to be met but a means of expressing our true Divine nature, in whatever way comes out most fluidly to us as individuals. We have all been bestowed with very unique skills, and those gifts are the fountain from which our creativity flows. But in a quest to *fit in* or *get it right,* many of us don't fully allow ourselves to tune into these gifts.

We strive and struggle to fit a mould, but it is only when we remember that there is no bloody mould that we get to be who we really are.

That is when we fully attune to Our Divine Essence.

Whether you sing, dance, write, grow plants, fold paper, fold clothes, cook, organise, speak or teach, it's all creativity, so own it. Know that, the more you flex your creativity muscles, the more magic you will be co-creating in your life.

Nurture Your Life Force Energy

Life force energy, which is basically source energy, animates your physical form, and literally brings you to life, flowing through you and all living things. Without it, you can no longer sustain life in your body.

Although we have unlimited access to this life force energy (The Divine Flow), the human body can only hold so much within it.

It is, therefore, really imperative to keep it charged and notice when it is being drained from you. To become more aware of when that energy becomes depleted in your body and find ways to nurture it.

One way of doing this is to become really mindful for how you feel within yourself. Do you generally feel depleted and drained? Also consider what you have been giving your attention and energy to so far today. Are they things that inspire, motivate and lift you higher? Or things that make you feel less than worthy, envious or irritated?

Your job is to become really unapologetic about spending more time on focused on that which charges you.

This is such an important thing to become attuned to because, as Danielle LaPorte says: *your energy is your abundance,* and I couldn't agree more. Because, your energy is not only your life force but it is your point of attraction. Meaning that your energy (put another way, **your vibration**) determines what is attracted into your life.

That is not to say that, if you feel *bad,* you will attract *bad* things. **Remember there are no *bad* emotions.** But if you consistently feel out of alignment energy-wise, you **will** find that your life is reflecting this. It might not be in obvious ways and it might not even look like negative things happening. It could just be that you feel out of sync, stagnant and like nothing is flowing in the way it was. That's how energy works.

This is why really taking care of your energy is of utmost importance. You can do this by doing the things that fill your energetic cup. Things like eating foods that nourish you, being around people who support you rather than pull you down, getting out in nature, mediating, resting.

The list is endless but it is, in essence, doing those things that make you feel really good in mind, body and soul. It's doing those things that connect you back to the feeling of love and joy and safety. It's about avoiding those things that make you feel unloved, joyless and unsafe. Those things will deplete and drain the energy from your body in a shot. It can also be affected by the way you speak to yourself and how you allow yourself to be treated because these things affect the way you feel within yourself; any mistreatment of yourself is actually only ever a mistreatment of your energy.

Shine And Don't Give A Shite

"Once your inner dialogue tells you that you are loveable and safe, your energy will manifest a life that affirms that."

Jerome Braggs

Nurture Your Connection to Yourself

One of the most beautiful gifts we can give ourselves is the gift of ourselves. When was the last time you actually gave yourself your time? How often do you find yourself giving to everyone and everything that needs your attention whilst neglecting yourself?

Through the work I do with others, I have been met with reasons for not making time for self, such as:

I'm too busy
I would feel too selfish
I have to look after everyone else
I can't relax
I don't think I need to

The thing is, they are all just excuses that ultimately hold us back from something that so many of us fear: a deeper connection to self.

I want to assure you that I do not judge, though, because every single one of those reasons has also come from my lips.

I would do everything you could possibly think of to avoid being with myself.. I don't mean being *by* myself, because one of my favourite past-times has always being on my own, maybe to read or sleep or write etc.

But I discovered that there was a massive difference between being *by* myself and *being* with myself.

The latter allowed me to connect more deeply to who I am, what I was feeling and what was truly holding me back from owning my light, sharing my gifts and living life on my terms.

Taking the time to truly connect with yourself every day is not a luxury. It's a vital ingredient if you want to enrich your life experience and live a life that lights you up.

You may find that if you are avoiding being with yourself, you are actually avoiding connecting with what is going on underneath the surface for you. Perhaps, out of a fear of what could come up if you truly let yourself go that deep.

I totally understand that, but there is actually nothing more freeing than allowing ourselves to stop hiding from those parts of ourselves we are scared of seeing.

From my experience, it is only when I stared to connect with myself through meditation that I began to *know* myself on a much deeper level because it was only then that I was able to *access* myself on a deeper level. Of course, there are so many ways in which you can meditate and the most common hold-back I hear from those who want to meditate but struggle is: *I just can't seem to quiet my mind enough.*

That is because there is a belief that successful meditation can only come from attaining the ultimate level of inner stillness.

But what if the purpose of connecting to yourself through meditation is to create a space for yourself to notice whatever thoughts and feelings want to come up, rather than seeing the goal as needing to push them aside or stop them?

During meditation, I started to just sit and allow whatever wanted to present itself to do just that, but instead of engaging with my thoughts and feelings (and therefore disconnecting from the moment) I just sat and let them **be** for long enough for them to move through me.

I would come out of my meditation feeling lighter because I had released what I had been holding onto but unable to access during the day-to-day busyness of my mind.

Meditation has actually become such a beautiful way of stepping outside of the distractions that would otherwise pull me away from who I truly am, what I truly desire and what I truly feel.

Your connection to yourself is the most important connection you will ever have.

When you are truly connected to yourself, you speak and act and live from your heart. When you are truly connected to yourself, you share your gifts with the world and inspire and help others along the way.

When you are truly connected to yourself, you allow yourself to give and receive and thrive in magical ways, without apology.

In a world that sees value in taking action, getting stuff done, elbow grease and knuckling down, it can be hard to accept the tremendous power of just sitting and being. But I (and I know many others) can attest to this: when you take time every day to sit in peaceful reflection and go inwards, the most MAGICAL messages will be revealed to you.

You will KNOW why you feel the way you do.

You will KNOW what your biggest fears are and how you can begin to release them.

You will KNOW what you are here to do, and doing it will be so fun, light, effortless.

You will KNOW what aligned and inspired action to take to follow your path.

Most importantly you will begin to KNOW yourself because the busyness of life will no longer be able to mask who you really are.

You are a space of infinite possibility, of infinite potential, of infinite abundance, of infinite love, so when you connect to yourself through meditation, you will actually start to release that part of you that you know is not you. And you will naturally start to merge more into who you truly are, which is such a magical process because it's like letting go of something heavy to allow light to flow into your life.

It is through that commitment to connect with yourself, to look after yourself, to nurture your needs, and to trust that you will know you are more than worthy of your inner most desires, dreams and more.

Part Five

Expand

Expand Outside of Your Comfort Zone

The thing about following your heart and your dreams is that you have to consistently and persistently keep moving out of your comfort zone.

Even when you feel utterly terrified!

I know that can be the most uncomfortable thing ever but it really is the only way to keep growing and expanding. And the discomfort that you currently feel at the thought of going beyond where you have been will fade over time.

Because, like any emotion, fear is not permanent.

You only need to bring to mind something that you were once worried about doing and can now look back and realise it wasn't half as bad as you thought it would be. It just took for you to actually *do* the thing to know that!

So just remember that. On the days when staying in your comfort zone seems much more appealing than stepping out of it, just think how far you've already come and that you can go even further. Just embrace the fear and keep moving forward in the direction of your dreams no matter what.

"Don't let the fear of the unknown prevent you from trying new things. Your comprehension of The Universe and your place in it expands every time you try something new."

Mr. K Wardle

(aka: Dapper_Tramp)

Shine And Don't Give A Shite

"Live in the 24-hours you are in. Tomorrow doesn't exist and you can't change what happened yesterday."

Joan Ee

Expand into Your Deepest Knowing

One of my favourite spiritual teachers is Esther Hicks. If you have not heard of her, she is a channel who receives guidance from a group of non-physical teachers called Abraham.

Basically, she receives and shares guidance from energetic beings that are not in physical form.

That may sound totally bizarre, and to be honest, when I first started following the work of Abraham-Hicks (as their collaborative work is popularly known), I was as skeptical as the next person.

But *why* was I?

I mean, I'd had enough personal experience to know that more exists beyond what we can we perceive with our five senses (as I shared in the chapter about awakening my extra-sensory gifts). So why was it hard at first to believe that what Abraham-Hicks could be sharing was exactly in-line with what I knew to be true anyway?

For me, I think this boils down to the loop of second-guessing that so many on this path of awakening find themselves in.

It is hard to escape the bombardment of contrary messaging that is telling us to look outside of ourselves for guidance and towards that which only makes *logical* sense.

But, if you've been doing this work for a bit, you will know that it rarely ever makes sense -- not to the rational mind, anyway. That's because the mind's role is to make sense of everything, and if it can't, it will throw it out as nonsense.

I began to be drawn to spiritual teachers such as Abraham-Hicks, the late Wayne Dyer, Rebecca Campbell, Michael Bernard Beckwith, Jerome Braggs, Deepak Chopra, Lee Harris and Kyle Cease and so many more only when I was willing to move beyond logical knowing and trust the infinite knowing within my soul. What they teach resonates with me deeply and profoundly in ways that may not have when I was only able to digest what seemed *normal*.

My intuitive knowing way surpassed my rational mind, and it was only then that what I was learning started to make sense. It was no longer about trying to prove it, it was about feeling the truth of it and feeling how much it resonated at a heart and soul level. Then my mind started to catch up because evidence of the teaching was presenting itself to me day in, day out, and it became utterly illogical to *not* believe it! (funny how that works!)

The point is, your journey is not about taking anyone else's word for anything. It's about beginning to tune into the part of yourself that knows truth when it experiences it, and that is all that matters. The more you connect with yourself, the more obvious and undeniable it will be.

Now, some may put this down to some kind of cult-like brainwashing. *Surely it must be that! I mean, it doesn't make sense otherwise huh?!*

But history teaches us that so much of what is now considered *the norm* were once unexplainable phenomena that made **no sense** at all.

Do you recall the Wright brothers, the American aviation pioneers who are considered the first people to invent, build, and fly the world's first airplane? They were labelled as insane by some and were laughed at for daring to believe in such a notion as flight, but they knew something that so many could not compute with their logical minds. It is because of them (and inventors like them) that we now get to enjoy the huge benefits of aviation.

They refused to give up on what they knew was possible. And there is a part of you calling for you to trust in *your* truth, too, and you only get there by choosing to go way beyond that part of you that needs others to get your truth before you embody it. Sure, there will be those around you that will try and talk you out of believing what you know to be true. I have experienced my fair share of that, but honestly, it does not phase me anymore.

I am learning what it means to trust *my* inner guidance implicitly, which feels way more amazing than gaining someone else's approval! So, expand into that place of knowing and into that place where you have the courage to trust *your* inner guidance beyond what is considered rational and normal because that's where the magic of expansion truly resides.

Expand Beyond Your Limited Self

At some point along your journey you will reach a kind of fork in the road where you must choose to either continue walking the path of old or embrace your brand new story. The one where you get to live life as who you truly are.

This is the choice of stepping into the perspective of Your Infinite Self and letting go of The Limited Self and all of its perceived limitations. The shifting between Your Limited Self into Your Infinite Self will occur through the process seeing where you **limit** yourself.

You will notice any ways in which you are trying to feel secure through things outside of you (material possessions or status or validation from others) versus connecting to the infinite security that you have available inside you when you connect to yourself in this moment.

As you make this shift, you may feel scared to leave a part of you behind. But what I have discovered is that no parts of ourselves ever get left behind, we just integrate those aspects of us that once felt scared and limited, and we show them what is available when we allow ourselves to expand way beyond.

You may also find that people who you once felt deeply connected to begin to drift away from you, almost like you are leaving them behind also.

This is because often as you change our habits and beliefs and ways of being, you may no longer be able to relate to those around you, and they may not be able to relate to you either.

This can be terrifying, especially if it is someone close to you.

But it is a natural part of evolution and growth. It does not mean that the person will not have a place in your life anymore, but that you are walking your own paths, and that is fine.

A part of you may feel tempted to go back to old limited ways in order to stay connected to them but ask yourself why you would do that?

What benefit to you or them could possibly come from you deliberately engaging in patterns that limit you and make you feel less than you can be?

What could be possible if you just keep allowing yourself to expand and grow, trusting that everyone has their own journey and that you do not need to sabotage your expansion for any reason whatsoever.

You are Infinite. You are Divine. You are Source.

When you reawaken to that, you will allow yourself to fully own your expansion. And as you bask in the knowing that you are already whole, complete and pretty friggin' AWESOME, everything will conspire around you to prove this to you.

"You are a spirit of the Universe in a human body. You are a unique, one-time-only being. Your likelihood of being here is about 1 in 4 trillion. You have earned your place. You have every right to be here. To have hopes, dreams and aspirations. You deserve to be happy and fulfilled. In short, you are fully, unapologetically allowed to thrive. No justification needed."

Helen Rebello

Expand into the Magical Place of Allowing

Expansion can be a real struggle, but when we realise that it's expansion we are here for (and we loosen our grip on how it *should* be), it actually becomes pretty easy and fun.

But it will take for you to consciously allow it to be easier and drop any feelings of resistance to letting it be that way. It might not feel easy at first and you might wonder how you can do that but it starts with just knowing that it can be easier and you deserve for it to be.

Because, as they say, resistance is futile.

When you do the inner work of releasing whatever feels out of alignment or feels heavy, you will float. This includes making the decision to let go of any resentments and unforgiveness that you may be holding onto because that, too, is resistance, and it will block you from letting in the abundance and opportunities and wisdom and love that wants to flow to you.

Expanding into a place of allowing is about letting go of any notion that you have to struggle in order to be who you are and live the life you desire, because that is a fallacy.

Life *will* present you with challenges but you need not expect them at every twist and turn. If you find yourself focusing on how difficult things have been up until now, just take a breath and be willing to believe that it can be easier from here on out. That **you** have the capacity to allow that.

In order to allow more, you will have to ditch those beliefs and thoughts that say you can't or shouldn't or mustn't expect *too much*.

Your Infinite Self, like The Universe, is always expanding and your job is to allow yourself to expand, too. Your capacity to live a truly rich, vibrant and massively abundant life starts with knowing that you are made for that and much, much more.

As you grow and evolve and expand more into yourself, and as you allow your light to shine out into the world, you will naturally become a magnet for magic to flow back into your life

Ultimate freedom will be yours the moment you allow yourself to live your life to the max as opposed to worrying *if* you're allowed to live your life to the max.

There may be a part of you that has huge resistance to even believing that life could be that simple because, if it were, why would there be any struggle in the world at all?

And I feel you.

I know just how hard it can be to let go of the idea that things have to be difficult and that there is plenty of evidence in the world right now proving to me that life being as simple as *allowing* is an airy fairy notion.

But what I know for sure is that it absolutely does start with what you are willing to believe is possible for **you** right now. Not what has happened in the past. Not what is happening to others. Your power lies in focusing on *your* expansion and allowing others the right to do the same.

Otherwise, you are setting yourself up to resist the flow and you will feel the discomfort in that. Besides, the part of you that is in resistance is the part of you that has always believed that life is *supposed* to be limited and simply won't allow it to be any other way.

That little voice inside you might be piping up with: *Who the hell are you to give up the belief that life is meant to be a struggle? Who are you to want it to come so easily?*

All I know is generations upon generations have been programmed to believe that, as humans, we are ultimately powerless, flawed and limited. That we have to be victims to life rather than co-creators of it.

I ask you to consider what MAGIC we could create for generations to come if we started living from the truth that we are ALL inherently powerful, whole, complete and infinite?

It starts with allowing yourself to *be* that example.

And until you decide and declare beyond any doubt that you are 100000000% worthy of it, what you desire most will never truly be yours. It's really ok to want what you want. It's why you came. To experience the fullness of life in all its glory! So allow yourself to expand into The Divine Flow of The Universe and allow it to carry you into magical places.

"Open yourself up to receive and The Universe will shower you with endless possibilities."

Phoebe Milenkovic

Expand into the Frequency of Love

It is now widely accepted in the field of quantum physics that we are waaaaaay more than just our fleshy, bony bodies. Who we are cannot be encapsulated by the skin that houses our other organs. We are more than that. We are energy.

In fact, *everything* is energy and everything vibrates at a certain frequency (including us humans). There are lots and lots of amazing resources that outline all of this in more detail, but you really don't need a book to tell you this. You will feel it.

When you become really attuned to yourself, you will feel that flow of life moving through you, and if you are really sensitive to energy, you will probably have always felt it. The energy that flows through us (which I chatted about a few chapters back) is known as life force energy or chi or prana (as well as other names).

And we all have equal and unlimited access to this energy.

But when we allow ourselves to connect with and go with the flow of The Universe our energy vibrates at higher and higher frequencies. When you do, you will feel it in every fibre of your being.

Shine And Don't Give A Shite

So when I talk about allowing yourself to be who you really are, it actually goes even deeper than just being true to your calling and doing what lights you up; it's actually about allowing yourself to BE the vibration and the frequency of LOVE.

Life Force Energy, Source energy *is* LOVE ENERGY.

And it's through expanding into that frequency of LOVE as frequently as you can that your life will become incredible beyond measure.

Everything that you desire to create in your life can be created when you access the frequency of LOVE because that is the *essence* of Your Divine Essence.

We can do this in all the ways I have shared with you in previous chapters, which essentially always comes down to doing more of what fills you with that feeling of love and connection and joy and abundance.

It's about opening up your heart to give and receive the love that is waiting to flow to you, through you and from you.

It is why your continued journey of healing is essential. When we live in a state of unhealed trauma and unexpressed emotions, we block the energetic flow of love and, therefore, vibrate at a lower frequency than is available for us.

That's not to say that lower vibrations are bad or should be avoided because that is impossible. It is about being ok with releasing what feels heavy, what feels stuck and what has been preventing you from living at a higher frequency up until now.

Your personal vibrational frequency, your energetic field is your magnet and, because like attracts like, it will draw to you that which you are a vibrational match for.

Although, this is not something I would encourage you to dwell on or try to rationalise (trust me, I've been there!) But it *is* something I would invite you to explore for yourself.

And for all that is good and holy, please don't let yourself get caught up in the story that says: *Well, if it were that easy, we'd all be bloody billionaires* or *If this is true, why do bad things happen to good people?* or *Yeah right, I'll believe it when see it…*

I'm going to be totally honest with you. None of this can be explained or rationalised. I don't believe that we will ever fully understand the mysteries of life and why some things are so unfair and why shit things happen.

I used to let these exact reasons be the perfect excuse for me to stay small and not allow myself to access my full power and light. I suppressed so much of myself because I refused to believe that we humans have the power to create destruction as much as we do miracles.

It felt like buying into this *stuff* was like flipping the bird to those who are struggling and suffering in life, and for the version of me that had been there, too. I soon realised though that we *do* have that power as humans.

We have the power to connect to Our Divine Truth and through that, we do have the power to change the fucking world, and I will keep choosing *that* over the fear of being all that I am, any day of the week.

You using any reason not to expand will forever keep you in a place of resistance. If you wanna fully embody all that you are, you are gonna have to allow yourself to experience the truth of it first.

Just know that if you allow yourself to focus on your life and where you are right now, your life will begin to transform, and when it does, the lives around you will begin to be positively influenced by that.

This will take you being totally focused on where you might be giving your energy away to doubt or complaining or things that don't make you feel good. To *anything* that feels unloving.

Pay attention to what happens when you make a conscious decision to focus even just a bit more on what lights you up, and in as little as 24-hours, you will notice magical occurrences in your life. You can treat it like a game and see what happens when you choose to spend more of your time in that vibration of love.

I would also absolutely recommend that you read the books *E-Squared* and *E-Cubed* by Pam Grout as she is awesome at showing you how to play around with vibrational energy in fun ways. Playing is a surefire way to raise your vibrational energy and attract more of the things of that same frequency into your life.

That's the incredibly powerful effect of expanding into the vibration of love. You tune into your capacity to co-create magic in your life in the most incredible ways. You will soon see the evidence of that in your life and how your open heart becomes a magnet for an abundance of beautiful blessings.

But know that the frequency of love can only be sustained to the degree that you are allowing yourself to love yourself.

If you are focusing your love only on others or what you do or what you desire, that's all well and good, but what about you?

I was reading a Facebook post a while ago in which someone was berated for daring to talk about truly loving herself. In the comment section someone responded with how disgusted she was that this person was so focused on love for herself and had not mentioned her love for others.

Therein lies the problem. This misguided notion that, by loving yourself, you somehow must be a selfish, neglectful and indulgent cow, and that loving yourself means you automatically stop loving everyone else.

I mean, surely the only reason we are put on this planet is to put loving ourselves so far down the list that we drive ourselves into continued states of anguish and despair.

Of course it's only those who focus on serving others first without any regard for themselves that are the truly good people of the world.

I hope you can sniff my sarcasm because, quite frankly, I am ready to say fuck off with that bullshit.

We are NOT put on this planet to focus on how we can give, give, give whilst refusing to LOVE ourselves. We are here to be who we are and love ourselves fully, completely and without apology, because the truth is, we can only love others to the extent that we love ourselves. Plain and simple.

We may feel like we can bypass loving ourselves and instead focus all our energy on being the nicest most accommodating and loving version of ourselves to others but that is what a martyr would do.

It's not a humble thing to put loving ourselves on the back-burner. It is unfair and totally soul-destroying.

The Facebook comment that I read really opened my eyes to how much the narrative of *self-love is selfish* actually abounds, and I can say first-hand how damaging that is.

It leads to burn-out and disconnection and illness.

It leads to feelings of shame around wanting to feel good.

It also leads to a feeling of unworthiness, which, I believe, is precisely what can cause someone to look outside of themselves for validation and approval in the first place. After all, when we have the validation and approval of someone else, it feels a lot like love.

But it is a temporary fix because the validation and approval and love that you have been looking for all this time is **your own.** Besides, loving **yourself** fully and completely does not mean that you have less to give **others.**

Because LOVE is not a finite resource.

It never runs out.

If that were true, it would follow that a parent could not possibly have enough love to give to more than one child unless they gave less love to their first born.

You will soon see that the more you fill yourself up with love, the more you will be overflowing, and you will have so much to give you will not be able to contain yourself.

Have you ever been around someone who just has so much love for themselves that it pours out of them and overspills, not only to those around them, but into their work and into the world, like the ripple effect of a pebble hitting the surface of a lake. I have, and it is such a beautiful energy to be around.

Today I invite you to begin that journey of opening your heart and expanding in the frequency of love by extending that love to YOU first.

You might not even know what that looks like or what you need to do in order to love yourself but loving yourself is not about *doing*. It is a state of *being* and *feeling*.

It is about having that same compassion and appreciation and understanding and acceptance and non-judgement for yourself that you would for anyone you truly love.

In doing so, you will be opening your heart up in a way you may have never experienced before.

Just know that this is not a trap.

Love is not a scam.

It is the basis of who you are and your job is to remain open to giving it, to receiving it and to, most importantly, BEING it.

"The greatest manifestations come from the purest of open hearts. Never apologise for who you are. Stay strong and true to yourself because you are the master creator. Share your light and love with those open to receiving."

Bianca Mitchell-Cowie

Final Words

And Then She Was Free

After what felt like an eternity of resisting herself, she broke through, she broke free and she finally allowed herself to thrive.

She realised that, for at least one day too many, she'd held herself back from being who she truly was and shining in the way she knew she could.

She'd allowed stories from the past to shatter her reality, keeping her frozen in a place of fear for waaaay too long.

She'd allowed herself to shrink and dim and play small in order to be loved and accepted in ways that had splintered her soul.

Most importantly, she'd entertained the bullshit and let it take up residence in her heart.

So she chose to stop doing all of that. She chose to believe in herself and all that was possible for her. She chose to let go of the resistance. She chose to move the frig forward.

And she chose to never look back.

(ok, well, perhaps only to rejoice in *just* how far she'd come!)

To Your Continued Shining

Thank you so much for taking the time to read my book! I really hope that it has opened you up to a new sense of possibility for yourself and your life.

Writing it was definitely a labour of love for me and perhaps the single most challenging thing that I have *ever* done.

It has taken to reach into spaces that I have kept hidden so that I can speak with integrity rather than tell you one thing while doing the total opposite myself.

That is the power of actually being true to ourselves.

We get to actually see the parts of ourselves that we have kept locked away for all this time only to realise that, underneath it all, we are actually ok.

I hope that you continue your journey of seeing more and more the magic that is you because the world needs you, your gifts and your truth. I know just how shit scary that can be, but future you will massively thank you for making the decision to step out and follow your heart.

Know that the rewards that come from having the courage to own your light will be well worth the consistent commitment and continued courage you'll be required to keep bringing to the table.

But if you've just read this book and you are feeling seriously overwhelmed at the thought of the insurmountable mountain you have ahead of you, I want you to remember that just one step at a time is the only commitment you really need to make to create your dreams.

Just keep moving, and on those days where you feel yourself climbing backwards or staying still, be easy on yourself. Some days we just need to do what we need to do and be where we need to be. And be super grateful for the progress you have already made because it's all progress. Trust me, it's all progress.

Besides, the path to becoming more of who we are never ends because, just like The Universe, we are always expanding and growing, and there really is no end to that expansion.

Remember, the juice is in journey, and as long as you honour how far you've come with grace and gratitude, your magical path will continue to be illuminated for you.

Follow your intuition and trust yourself.

Even if it makes no sense (it will eventually).

Even if some may think you're odd (who wants to be normal?)

Even if others judge (because, let's face it, those who judge others for being themselves have lost their own damn way).

Even if your bright-bold-spirit triggers others, you have to keep choosing yourself over and over again.

At some stage along the way, you are gonna stop, take a gasp and realise just how wonderful you really are.

You will suddenly be open, with wide-eyed wonder, to the beauty of who you are, and you will know exactly why those who love you, just as you are, adore you so.

You will feel the overwhelming sense of love for yourself that you were born with; it will finally return and then, in that moment, you will rejoice in the awesomeness that is YOU, and you will never, ever, forget again.

So, my advice is, always be yourself.

Make a decision to be truer to yourself today than you were yesterday.

Believe in yourself implicitly.

Have full faith that what you desire for yourself and your life is already yours.

Follow what makes your heart sing and embrace your dreams with passion.

But most of all remember to keep on shining.

All my love,

Magical Life Contract

I hereby give my permission for everything in my life, from here on in, to be more magical than I could possibly imagine.

I let the order of my days (from this one forward) to be so filled to the brim with happiness, abundance, fun and joy that my cheeks will ache from all of the smiling and laughing that they will be supporting.

I give up any grudges, resentments, negative beliefs and self-sabotaging behaviours. I finally surrender to the truth of who I am. Not who I, or anyone else by that matter, feel I should be. I rejoice in my choices and my desires, knowing and trusting that, as long as I follow my own inner truth, I shall never be led astray.

Last but certainly not least, I intend to make my dominant vibration one of sheer appreciation for all of the blessings that have been, and are yet to be, bestowed upon my life.

In gratitude,

(Your Name)

Massive Heartfelt Thanks

I am beyond grateful for the sheer magnitude of love and encouragement from those who believed I could write this book long before I believed I could! Thank you x10000000!

To my family and friends who have supported me in my journey, I am so thankful to have you in my life.
Thank you so much to my beautiful soul sisters, Maria and Krystal-Anne who, without judgement, lovingly held space for me whilst I ironed out the doubts and fears that arose in the days, weeks and months that I was actually writing this book.

Thank you to lovely Jasmyne for her incredible (and much needed!) proof-reading skills and my amazing mum, Mary who helped with formatting when I was ready to throw my laptop out of the window!

And…thank you to Enrico for your tremendous support during the 18 months it took me to complete this project. Beyond that, thank you for 18 years of never trying to change me or diminish my dreams. Thank you for giving me the space to evolve and grow as I have walked a path you may not have understood, and for trusting in me even when I didn't quite have it all figured out. You truly deserve a medal. ☺

Shine And Don't Give A Shite

Acknowledgements

Special thanks to those who have contributed to the creation of my book through their beautiful images and their words of wisdom! You can find out more about the contributors through the websites associated with their work (where applicable).

Photo Credits:

Front Cover - credit to max-kegfire on www.istock.com

Page 20 - credit to Jack B on www.unsplash.com

Page 36 - credit to it's me neosiam on www.pexels.com

Page 46 - credit to Myriams-Fotos on www.pixabay.com

Page 54 - credit to fotografierende on www.pexels.com

Page 62 - credit to rawpixel.com on www.pexels.com

Page 74 - credit to Fröken Fokus on www.pexels.com

Page 81 - credit to Ben White on www.unsplash.com

Page 93 - credit to Porapak Apichodilok on www.pexels.com

Page 111 - credit to Levi Saunders on www.unsplash.com

Page 121 - credit to nappy on www.pexels.com

Page 133 - credit to Wellington Cunha on www.pexels.com

Page 144 - credit to Edu Carvalho on www.pexels.com

Page 148 - credit to Giulia Bertelli on www.unsplash.com

Page 161 - credit to Dids on www.pexels.com

Page 177 - credit to Daniel Angele on www.unsplash.com

Page 204 - credit to Burak K on www.pexels.com

Page 219 - credit to andrew Roberts on www.pexels.com

Page 232 - credit to Markus Spiske on www.unsplash.com

Page 239 - credit to Ihsan Aditya on www.pexels.com

Page 248 - credit to rawpixel.com on www.pexels.com

Page 257 - credit to Simon Migaj on www.unsplash.com

Page 264 - credit to Oleksandr Pidvalnyi on www.pexels.com

Page 269 - credit to Abhiram Prakash on www.pexels.com

Page 279 - credit to Victor Freitas on www.pexels.com

Page 290 - credit to Caio Resende on www.pexels.com

Shine And Don't Give A Shite

Quotation Credits:

Wilferd Peterson

Norman Vincent Peale

Abraham Maslow

Jim Rohn

Rumi

Johann Wolgang von Goethe

Joan Ee

Napoleon Hill

Anaïs Nin

Charles Bukowski

Keeley Nicholls - www.soulvibesanctuary.com

Debbie McDermott - www.debbie-mcdermott.com

Jessica Jones - www.thefatfunnyone.com

Kyle Cease - www.kylecease.com

Jacob Nordby - www.blessedaretheweird.com

Hannah Mang - www.hannahmang.com

Rebecca Campbell - www.rebeccacampbell.me

Krystal-Anne Smith - www.fb.com/spirituallotuswellness

Brooke Hampton - www.barefootfive.com

Maria Mara - www.goddessgrounded.com

Annika Spalding - www.annikaspalding.co.uk

Depika Mistry - www.anoume.com

Lee Harris - www.leeharrisenergy.com

Helen Rebello - www.helenrebello.com

Mike Dooley - www.tut.com

Brené Brown www.brenebrown.com

Danielle LaPorte - www.daniellelaporte.com

Jerome Braggs - www.jeromebraggs.com

Mr K Wardle - www.instagram.com/dapper_tramp

Phoebe Milenkovic - www.facebook.com/sacreddevotion

Bianca Mitchell-Cowie - www.mummawellness.com

Gina Hatzis - www.ginahatzis.com

Natasha K Benjamin - www.instagram.com/natashakbenjamin

Magical Resources

Ok, so I didn't wanna leave you hanging, so here is a (condensed!) list of some of the books I have read and resources that I would highly recommend for your onward journey of owning your light, sharing your gifts and living a truly magical life.

Awesome Books:

Be Your Own Life Coach by Fiona Harrold

The Miracle Morning by Hal Elrod

The Untethered Soul by Michael A. Singer

Light is the New Black by Rebecca Campbell

Rise Sister Rise by Rebecca Campbell

The Magic Path of Intuition by Florence Scovel Shinn

You Are a Badass by Jen Sincero

Your Place of Power by Dr Michael Bernard Beckwith

You Can Heal Your Life by Louise L Hay

Manifest Your Destiny by Dr Wayne Dyer

The Big Leap by Gay Hendricks

Change Your Thoughts, Change Your Life by Dr Wayne Dyer

The Four Agreements by Don Miguel Ruiz

The Magic by Rhonda Byrne

The Secret by Rhonda Byrne

The Power by Rhonda Byrne

Thank and Grow Rich by Pam Grout

Loving What Is by Byron Katie

The Seven Spiritual Laws of Success by Deepak Chopra

Lucky Bitch by Denise Duffield-Thomas

Excuse Me, Your Life Is Waiting by Lynn Grabhorn

Don't Sweat the Small Stuff by Richard Carlson

Ask and it is Given by Esther & Jerry Hicks

Money & the Law of Attraction by Esther & Jerry Hicks

The Vortex by Esther & Jerry Hicks

Blessed are the Weird by Jacob Nordby

The Rules of Life by Richard Templar

The Soul Connection by Anne Jones

The Life-Changing Magic of Not Giving a F**k by Sarah Knight

What if This is Heaven by Anita Moorjani

Feel Free to Prosper by Marilyn Jenett

Energy Speaks by Lee Harris

Incredible Distant Healers

Brad Yates (Awesome EFT Practitioner) - www.bradyates.net

Keeley Nicholls (Quantum Energy Healer) -
www.soulvibesanctuary.com

Alix McGill (Intuitive reader, Reiki Healer & Tarot Reader) -
mcgillalix@gmail.com

Depika Mistry (Intuitive, Energy Healer) - www.anoume.com

Christie-Marie Sheldon (Intuitive Energy Healer) -
www.christiesheldon.com

Krystal-Anne Smith (Spiritual Empowerment Mentor &
Reiki Master) www.fb.com/spirituallotuswellness

Jerome Braggs (Energy Intuitive & Healer) -
www.jeromebraggs.com

About Kirsty

Kirsty Caló is a mum, singer, writer, artist, teacher and mentor who loves creating awesome things that inspire those who've lost their way reawaken their inner magic.

You can find out more about her work at
www.kirstycalo.com

"We SHINE not for your adoration. We SHINE because, baby, you can't dim the sun."

Gina Hatzis

(#TooMuchWomanMovement)

Printed in Great Britain
by Amazon

57025814R00174